U.S. Navy Flying and Amphibians in World War II

Al Adcock

Squadron Signal Publications

Cover painting and profiles by Don Greer

Acknowledgements

Tailhook Association (Tailhook)
Naval Historical Center
Cmdr. Doug Seigfried,
    U.S. Navy (Ret.)
NASA
U.S. National Archives
U.S. Navy
Real War Photos
David Sconyers
U.S. Coast Guard

Igor Sikorsky Historical Archives
Dan Libertino
Bill Tuttle
Consolidated Aircraft
Martin Aircraft
Northrop Grumman Archives
Chief Petty Officer Mike Johnson,
    U.S. Navy
San Diego Aerospace Museum
    (SAM)

A very special thanks to Doug Siegfried at the Tailhook Association for his valued help on this title. His enthusiasm and knowledge of U.S. Navy aircraft went a long way to helping me with "building" this book. Thanks, Doug.

About the Special Series

Squadron/Signal Publications' most open-ended genre of books, our Special category features a myriad of subjects, including unit histories, military campaigns, aircraft, ships, armor, and uniforms. Upcoming subjects include war heroes and nonmilitary areas of interest.

Copyright 2008 Squadron/Signal Publications

1115 Crowley Drive
Carrollton, TX 75006 U.S.A.

Printed in the U.S.A.

www.SquadronSignalPublications.com

ISBN 978-0-89747-556-3

If you have any photographs of aircraft, armor, soldiers, or ships of any nation, particularly wartime snapshots, please share them with us and help make Squadron/Signal's books all the more interesting and complete in the future. Any photograph sent to us will be copied and returned. Electronic images are preferred. The donor will be fully credited for any photos used. Please send them to:

Squadron/Signal Publications Inc.
1115 Crowley Drive
Carrollton, TX 75006 U.S.A.

Front cover: The pilot runs up the engine as the radio operator/observer makes his way into the rear cockpit of a U.S. Coast Guard Grumman JF-2 preparing to make a patrol flight in 1940. The amphibian Duck performed search-and-rescue, liaison, and photographic duties for the U.S. Navy and the U.S. Coast Guard during World War II. (*Tailhook*)

Title page: Three Douglas PD-1s from Patrol Squadron 4F (VP-4F) fly in the vicinity of Oahu, Territory of Hawaii, in 1936. Douglas Aircraft was known for building transports and bombers during and after World War II. The PD-1 was powered by Wright Cyclone R-1750 engines and had a wingspan of 72 feet. (*Tailhook*)

Back cover top: A Consolidated PBY-5A Catalina from Patrol Squadron 31 (VP-31) has its right engine inspected in 1943. The eighth aircraft in the squadron, it is equipped with radar on the wing undersides. (*Tailhook*)

Back cover bottom left: A Martin PBM-1 Mariner from Patrol Squadron 56 (VP-56) flies over Maryland in 1941. A neutrality star is painted on the nose, and a portion of the top of the wings is yellow-orange. The Mariner was armed with five .50-caliber machine guns. (*Tailhook*)

Back cover bottom right: A U.S. Navy aviator is delivered to the Grumman Bethpage flight line to pick up a new JRF-5 Goose utility transport amphibian in the summer of 1943. The little Grumman is camouflaged in the tri-tone scheme adopted in 1943. (*Tailhook*)

Introduction

When early aviation pioneers first learned to fly, they turned their attention to water because it was more abundant than land and presented a vast landing area.

Water, however, proved to be a more difficult medium than first thought, and it was not until 1905, two years after the Wright brothers' first flight, that Frenchman Gabriel Vosin made a successful flight from water, albeit from a towed glider. The Vosin brothers then designed a powered flying boat and, following flight tests that did not meet their expectations, abandoned the project.

Early American aviation enthusiast and aircraft designer Glenn H. Curtiss added floats to his June Bug and made his first flight from water in November 1908. The little craft was only able to make about 25 mph and was unstable. Curtiss abandoned further tests. He then designed his Model D, which, with a modified canoe as a float, made many successful flights.

Glenn Curtiss, though, will be forever remembered for his Hydoaeroplane, for which he received a patent in 1911. Curtiss asked his old friend Charles F. Pond, the captain of the USS *Pennsylvania* (ACR-4) to allow him to fly out to the ship and land beside the armored cruiser. Curtiss taxied up to the ship, and the ship's boat crane was used to bring the flying boat aboard. This concept allowed the U.S. Navy to develop the shipboard floatplanes that would be so important during World War II.

During World War I, the Curtiss Aeroplane and Engine Co. produced F-Boats for training and the HS, H-12, and H-16 for anti-submarine patrols. The U.S. Navy entered the war flying Curtiss' flying boats exclusively. The British also operated Curtiss' boats and improved on their design. The Curtiss flying boats were the only American-designed aircraft to see combat in the European conflict.

The Curtiss NC flying boats, called Nancy Boats, were finished too late to see action during the war but were used to make the first crossing of the Atlantic in 1919. Four flying boats, NC-1 through NC-4, took off from the United States and flew to Europe. One aircraft, NC-4, was the only aircraft able to complete the flight across the Atlantic.

The Wright brothers also got into the seaplane business in 1914 when they tested their Model G, a flying boat designed by Grover Loening under the supervision of Orville Wright. The Model G was the only flying boat developed by the Wright Co. Grover Loening would go on to start his own aircraft company, and he designed the Loening OL-5, which would be used as the basis for the Grumman JF-1 Duck amphibian.

Following World War I, the U.S. Navy turned its attention to the new aircraft carrier USS *Langley* (CV-1), the converted collier USS *Jupiter*, the first ship powered by electric motor. The *Langley* was the host to many early aircraft constructed by Boeing, Curtiss, Grumman, Loening, and Douglas. She was sunk by Japanese naval aviation off Java on 27 February 1942, not long after the Pearl Harbor raid.

The U.S. Navy, between the wars, continued to seek newer patrol planes and accepted designs from Boeing Aircraft, Douglas Aircraft, Consolidated Aircraft, Hall Aluminum, Glenn L. Martin Aircraft Co., and the Naval Aircraft Factory (NAF). Up to 1928, water-cooled engines had been used on all U.S. Navy patrol planes, until the NAF rebuilt a Boeing PB-1 with Pratt & Whitney R-1690 air-cooled radial engines, replacing the Packard water-cooled engine and changing the designation to XPB-2.

Two companies made radial engines: Wright Aeroplane and Engine Co. and Pratt & Whitney, a division of United Aircraft. Radial engines had the advantage of being lighter, not requiring coolant, and having high sustained-power ratings. The radial engine required precision parts to function correctly, and only two manufacturers could produce the high-powered engines required by the military. The radial engine proved itself during World War II when aircraft returned to base with many of the cylinders, called "jugs," missing and the engine still running.

U.S. Navy flying boats and amphibians wore various color schemes from World War I through World War II. During the first war, U.S. Navy patrol bomber aircraft were painted a dark Navy gray, some with light gray stripes as a means of camouflage. After the war, patrol aircraft were painted in an overall aluminum dope. In 1925, the Bureau of Aeronautics (BuAir) issued a directive that all patrol planes have the top of the wing and horizontal stabilizers painted a chrome yellow for visibility in case the aircraft was forced down on the water. The scheme was used until 1941, when patrol planes were painted in a short-lived overall light gray camouflage. By 1942, all patrol and amphibians were camouflaged in a nonspecular (NS) blue-gray over NS light gray. In 1943, a tri-tone scheme of NS sea blue and NS intermediate blue over a NS insignia white was used. The final World War II scheme required all aircraft operating in combat zones to be painted an overall gloss Navy blue. Some exceptions existed, of course, such as the PBY Catalina squadrons in the South Pacific that were painted in an overall black scheme and called the Black Cats. Some experiments used greens and various other shades of blue; but, for the most part, the BuAir directives were followed, although not always to the letter.

U.S. Navy flying boats, seaplanes, and amphibians provided valuable service to both World War I and II efforts and would continue to serve with the U.S. Navy and U.S. Coast Guard until the war in Vietnam, when the last P5M Marlin squadron was decommissioned. The flying boats and amphibians were replaced by helicopters and land-based patrol bombers.

The Loening OL-5 was the first aircraft purchased by the U.S. Coast Guard and was used at Gloucester, Massachusetts, in 1926. A 435-horsepower inverted V-1650 Liberty engine powered the OL-5. The OL-5 carried U.S. Coast Guard aircraft number 3 until it was renumbered to V103 before World War II. The OL-5 formed the basis for the Grumman JF-1 Duck. (*USCG*)

Boeing

The Boeing Airplane Co. was founded by William E. "Bill" Boeing in Seattle, Washington, in 1915. The Boeing Co. was originally called the Pacific Aero Products Co. with the sole purpose of producing airplanes. The first aircraft produced by Boeing was the Model 1 (B&W), the "B" standing for Boeing and the "W" for Conrad Westervelt, a Navy officer who was assigned to a local U.S. Navy shipyard and was instrumental in forming the Pacific Aero Products Co. The Model 1 was a biplane utility seaplane powered by a 100-horsepower Hall-Scott A-5 water-cooled inline engine. The Model 1 design closely followed that of a Martin seaplane that Bill Boeing had purchased to study the construction methods of aircraft.

Boeing would continue to improve on the design of seaplanes. The company would gain notoriety, however, by building fighter planes and bombers for the U.S. Army and Navy during the 1920s and '30s. Boeing also produced the first successful commercial airliner, the Model 247 monoplane. The 247 was a development of the Boeing B-9 bomber and the Monomail. The Model 247 was the first in the many successful commercial airline designs that would come out of the assembly plants in Seattle and Renton, Washington.

Although known for producing the B-17 Flying Fortress and B-29 Superfortress, Boeing would produce four flying boat designs that would be used by the U.S. Navy during World War II. The first was the Boeing Model 314 flying boat. The 314 was ordered by Pan Am for its Pacific and Atlantic routes. The original order was for six aircraft, all called Clippers, with the first being the Honolulu Clipper. The Model 314 used the wings and engine nacelles from the Boeing B-19 bomber and a large flying boat hull. When completed, the 314 was the largest production airplane in commercial service. Its first flight was on 7 June 1938, and following test flights, the Model 314 was cleared for passenger service.

Pan Am was impressed by the Model 314 and ordered an additional six aircraft, designated the 314A, with improvements in range and performance. When World War II began for the United States, the U.S. Navy and Army purchased nine of the 314As and the British Purchasing Commission purchased three. The U.S. Navy contracted Pan Am to operate the 314; some were operated in civilian markings and some were camouflaged and carried civilian registrations. All of the U.S. Navy aircraft were assigned bureau numbers. The U.S. Army designated the 314 as the C-98 and in 1943 gave its 314s to the U.S. Navy and one to Pan Am. One 314 sank on 14 November 1945 when it lost an engine 700 miles from Honolulu, Hawaii. The Honolulu Clipper landed in the Pacific, and while the seaplane tender USS *San Pablo* (AVP-30) was attempting to take it in tow, the 314A crashed into the ship. The damage was serious enough to cause the aircraft to be sunk by gunfire so it would not present a hazard to navigation.

The XPBB-1 was ordered by the U.S. Navy in 1940 and first flown in 1942. As constructed, the XPBB-1 was the largest twin-engine flying boat of World War II. Powered by a pair of 2,000-horsepower Wright R-3350-8 Double-Compound radial engines, the Sea Ranger was to be built at the new U.S. Navy facility constructed at Renton, Washington, especially to build the XPBB-1. The U.S. Navy, however, decided that the B-29 bomber was more important than another flying boat and decided to build the Superfortress at the Renton plant. The single XPBB-1, now called the Lone Ranger, spent most of the war at Naval Air Station Norfolk performing search-and-rescue and patrol duties.

Boeing of Canada constructed the final two flying boats, derivatives of the Consolidated PBY Catalina. A total of 240 PB2B-1s were constructed, with the majority going to the Royal Australian Air Force, Royal Air Force, and the Royal New Zealand Air Force. The PB2B-1 was essentially a duplicate of the Consolidated PBY-5.

Boeing also produced a version of the Consolidated PBY-6A and Naval Aircraft Factory PBN-1 Nomad, designated the PB2B-2. The PB2B-2 featured a taller tail, and most were fitted with search radar in a housing over the cockpit area. Boeing of Canada, Montreal, also produced 55 duplicates of the amphibian Consolidated PBY-5A, with all going to the Royal Canadian Air Force. It was unusual that a Boeing designator was not used for the Canadian-produced PBY-5A.

A Pan American Airways System (Pan Am) Boeing Model 314A, the Honolulu Clipper, is docked at Alameda, California, in 1940. The aircraft would soon be purchased by the U.S. Navy and given the bureau number (BuNo) 48227. The aircraft would be operated by Pan Am carrying the civilian registration NC18801. (*William T. Larkins via SAM*)

Above: The Honolulu Clipper founders in the Pacific Ocean north of Hawaii on 14 November 1945, following a fire and loss of the left inboard engine. The small seaplane tender USS *San Pablo* (AVP-30) attempted to take the 314A in tow, but the aircraft crashed into the ship, causing considerable damage, and the Model 314A had to be sunk. (*Real War Photos*)

Right: The Yankee Clipper, a Pan Am Boeing Model 314A, makes a takeoff run in 1941. Purchased by the U.S. Navy in 1942, the aircraft was given the bureau number 48224, flown in civilian markings, and registered as NC18603 so it could enter neutral ports during World War II. The Yankee Clipper crashed in the River Tagus, Lisbon, Portugal, on 22 February 1943. (*Tailhook*)

Below: The Pan Am Atlantic Clipper sits at dock on 5 October 1939, carrying civilian markings NC18604. The U.S. Navy purchased the aircraft in 1942, and the Boeing Model 314A was assigned the bureau number 48225. It was operated by Pan Am during the war. Following the war, the Atlantic Clipper was salvaged for parts. (*National Archives*)

Above: The Dixie Clipper was purchased by the U.S. Navy in 1942 and was operated by Pan Am until the end of the war. President Franklin Roosevelt used the Dixie Clipper to fly to the Casablanca Conference in January 1943, becoming the first in-office president to fly and making the aircraft the first presidential aircraft, Navy One. (*Elsilrac*)

Left: The Dixie Clipper shares the harbor at Pearl City, Territory of Hawaii, on 6 June 1944 with a pair of Martin PBM Mariners. The Boeing Model 314A is camouflaged in an unusual scheme that appears to be NS medium blue and NS blue-gray over NS light gray. The American flag is painted on the forward fuselage and the center vertical stabilizer. (*National Archives*)

Below: The British Purchasing Commission ordered three Boeing Model 314As in April 1941, and they were operated by British Overseas Airways Corp. G-AGBZ was named the Bristol and was camouflaged in an extra dark sea gray and dark slate gray over night scheme. The Speedbird emblem is placed on the nose below the aircraft name. The British Union Jack also shares the nose area. (*SAM*)

The Pacific Clipper, a Boeing Model 314A, was delivered to Pan Am in May 1941, purchased by the U.S. Navy in 1942, and assigned the bureau number 48228. It was flown in camouflage with civilian markings by Pan Am crews with the obligatory American flag on the nose and the center vertical stabilizer. The civilian registration NC18609 appeared on the outer vertical stabilizers and on the lower-left wing and the upper-right wing. (*SAM*)

The Boeing XPBB-1 was, at the time of its introduction, the largest twin-engine flying boat ever built. The Boeing Model 344 sits on beaching gear before its first flight on 9 July 1942 at Renton, Washington. The XPBB-1 is camouflaged in the then-standard scheme of NS blue-gray over NS light gray. (*Tailhook*)

The XPBB-1 (BuNo 3144) has been launched, and a boat has been pulled alongside to deliver the flight crew. The XPPB-1 was powered by a pair of Wright Duplex Cyclone R-3350 two-row radial engines that produced 2,000 horsepower for takeoff. Its maximum speed was rated at 219 mph, and it had a service ceiling of 18,900 feet. (*Tailhook*)

Above: The XPBB-1 makes its first flight from Lake Washington in 1942. The XPBB-1 was officially designated as Sea Ranger, and it was expected that following a successful flight a production contract would be forthcoming. The U.S. Navy had other ideas, however, and no contracts were issued, making the Sea Ranger the Lone Ranger. (*Tailhook*)

Left: The XPBB-1 has now been armed, with eight .50-caliber machine guns, a pair mounted in the nose, dorsal, and tail powered turrets, and a single gun in the manually operated waist turrets. The XPBB-1 had a wingspan of 139 feet and a length of 94 feet. Endurance was rated at 72 hours, a phenomenal range for such a large aircraft. (*Tailhook*)

Below: In the summer of 1943, the XPBB-1 was camouflaged in a different scheme, and a new red surround with white bars was placed on the national insignia. The Boeing Wing Design 117 that was used on the XPBB-1 was adapted for the Boeing B-29 Superfortress. The maximum gross takeoff weigh, when using jet-assisted takeoff (JATO) rockets, was 101,129 pounds, and the normal range was 4,245 miles at economical cruise speed. (*Tailhook*)

Above: Following testing, the XPBB-1 was flown overland to Naval Air Station Norfolk, Virginia, where the Sea Ranger performed various duties, such as patrol and air-sea rescue. Following the war, the aircraft was broken up and salvaged for the various metals and components, thus ending the career of the largest twin-engine flying boat of World War II. (*Tailhook*)

Right: Boeing built 67 PB2B-2 Catalina VIs, which were a version of the Naval Aircraft Factory PBN-1. The PB2B-2 had a modified vertical stabilizer, a nose turret that housed a pair of .30-caliber machine guns, and a radome mounted atop the cockpit. A pair of Pratt & Whitney R-1830-92 radial engines powered the PB2B-2. (*SAM*)

Below: The Royal Australian Air Force received 46 PB2B-2s, such as this example, OX-V (BuNo 124752), that served with No. 43 Black Cat Squadron Queensland, Northern Territory. The PB2B-2s were painted overall a dull black with the squadron codes in a light gray. The Australians received their first PBY-5 Catalinas in 1940. (*Elsilrac*)

Consolidated Aircraft

Consolidated Aircraft was formed by Maj. Reuben Fleet in 1923 when he purchased the Gallaudet Aircraft Corp. and the rights to the Dayton-Wright Co. designs from General Motors. During World War I, many automobile companies began designing or producing aircraft, but following the war most returned to building automobiles.

Maj. Fleet was instrumental in forming the U.S. Air Mail Service and designing the military parachute. A pilot himself, he saw the need for a reliable trainer plane for the U.S. Army and designed the PT-1 Trusty primary trainer. Many designs would follow, but none was more famous than the Consolidated PBY Catalina.

The predecessor to the PBY was the Consolidated XPY-1 and the P2Y. The XPY-1 was a twin-engine flying boat. The first one, though, had a third engine mounted above the wing. Tests showed little performance increase, and the engine was removed. Glenn L. Martin Aircraft underbid Consolidated for the contract, and it built the XPY-1 as the P3M-1 for the U.S. Navy. The P2Y was also a twin-engine flying boat but was designed as a sesquiplane. The P2Y-1 exhibited outstanding performance and range. Foreign sales were made to Argentina, Columbia, and Japan.

In 1933, the U.S. Navy ordered a prototype flying boat that would become a household name around the world — Catalina. The XP3Y-1 would become the most widely produced patrol bomber of World War II, with production undertaken in the United States, Canada, and Russia. The XP3Y-1 was a high-wing (parasol type) all-aluminum design, with the exception of some canvas just behind the main spar to the trailing edge. A pair of R-1830-58 Pratt & Whitney Twin-Wasp 14-cylinder radial engines powered the XP3Y-1. The design was a complete departure from the earlier biplane design, and it incorporated aerodynamic features such as folding wingtip floats, a streamlined fuselage, and a bow-mounted gun turret. The XP3Y-1 was partially assembled at Consolidated's Buffalo, New York, facility and shipped by rail to Naval Air Station Norfolk, Virginia, for assembly and flight testing.

The Consolidated Aircraft factory had been moved to Lindbergh Field, San Diego, California, in late 1935 to enable flight testing of aircraft all year. The XP3Y-1 designator was changed to reflect its role as a patrol bomber, and the PBY-1 Catalina was put into production. Orders for the PBY-2, 3, and 4 followed. In December 1939, the U.S. Navy ordered 200 of the PBY-5 model, the largest single aircraft order since World War I. Many thousands would follow when the United States entered World War II in December 1941.

The PBY-5 was similar to the earlier models with a few exceptions. A pair of glass enclosures were fitted for the waist gunners, and R-1830-82 engines were installed that could burn 100-octane fuel.

The PBY-5 was further modified with amphibian gear that would enable the aircraft to operate from land as well as water. This modification greatly enhanced the utility of the Catalina. The last production PBY-4 (BuNo 1245) was used as a test aircraft for tricycle gear. The nose gear folded up under the cockpit area, and the main wheels folded into the fuselage sides. The combined weight of the tricycle gear was 2,300 pounds, and this reduced maximum speed from 195 mph to 179 mph. Maximum gross weight rose to 35,500 pounds. The Catalina was designed for range, not speed, and the PBY-5 series had a maximum range of 2,800 miles, or 28 hours at 100 mph cruising speed.

The last PBY was the PBY-6A, a PBY-5A with a modified tail adopted from the Naval Aircraft Factory PBN-1. The PBY-6A had a bow-mounted turret with a pair of .30-caliber machine guns and a radome over the cockpit area that housed a surface search radar antenna. When the last PBY-6A rolled off the assembly line at New Orleans in September 1945, a total of 3,281 Catalinas had been produced in the United States. Boeing of Canada, Vickers of Canada, and Russia also added to the production figures.

The U.S. Navy, however, wanted a larger patrol bomber and put out a request for proposal for a large four-engine flying boat that had speed, range, and defensive armament. Both Sikorsky and Consolidated submitted proposals and prototype aircraft for evaluation. The Consolidated XPB2Y-1 was chosen over Sikorsky's entrant, the XPBS-1. The XPB2Y-1 was originally flown with a single tail, but flight tests indicated a directional stability problem, and the aircraft was fitted with twin vertical stabilizers, much in the fashion of the Consolidated B-24 bomber that was introduced in 1939. The XPB2Y-1 served as the flag plane for the commander of the Aircraft Scouting Force during the war in the Pacific.

Following flight tests, six PB2Y-2 Coronados were ordered and assigned to Patrol Squadron 13 (VP-13) for flight training. The PB2Y-3 followed with a production run of 136 models. A low-powered version, the PB2Y-5 was developed to increase range. Many of the -3 and -5 models were modified as transports as the U.S. Navy found that land-based Consolidated B-24s and PB4Ys proved just as useful in the patrol bomber role.

Consolidated was purchased in 1943 by Vultee Aircraft, and the new combined company was called Consolidated-Vultee Aircraft, or Convair. In 1954, the name was changed to General Dynamics, since the company ventured into making of submarines when Convair and Electric Boat merged.

Consolidated P2Y-2 Ranger from Patrol Squadron 15 (VP-15) makes a patrol flight in 1939. The P2Y-2 was considered a sesquiplane, since the lower wing did not equal the span of the upper wing. This craft, 15 P-7, was the section leader of the third element and carried full red cowlings and a red fuselage stripe. VP-15 was established at Kaneohe, Territory of Hawaii, in 1936. (*Tailhook*)

A Patrol Squadron 10F (VP-10F) P2Y-2 Ranger (10-P-5) taxis to take off from San Francisco, California, in February 1935 in a record-setting flight to Hawaii. The five-plane formation, assigned to Patrol Wing 1, took 24 hours to fly the 2,400-mile journey. This P2Y-2 had black stripes on the horizontal and vertical stabilizers. (*Tailhook*)

A parade of 1939-era Lincoln and Cadillac automobiles passes by a P2Y-3 assigned to the commander of Patrol Squadron 43 in 1941. The aircraft 43-P-1 was the last P2Y-3 assigned to Naval Air Station Jacksonville and the last P2Y-3 in squadron service. The neutrality star has been placed on the nose for recognition. (*Tailhook*)

Above: The beaching crew struggles to align a P2Y-2 from Training Squadron 2 (VN-2) at Naval Air Station Pensacola in 1941. Aircraft No. 18 has its horizontal and vertical stabilizers painted in insignia red. The beaching crew will affix the beaching gear that would allow the P2Y-2 to be placed on land. All of the control cables on the empennage are exposed. (*Tailhook*)

Left: Aviation cadets at Naval Air Station Pensacola look on as the engines of a P2Y-3 are run up. The aircraft was formally serving in squadron service as the third aircraft in the section flight. The P2Y aircraft employed an extensive array of supports and struts for the two wings. The P2Ys were powered by Wright R-1820 twin-row radial engines. (*Tailhook*)

Below: The crew members of a P2Y-3 deplanes via a portable ramp so as not to get their feet wet. The P2Y was assigned to Training Squadron 4 (VN-4) at Naval Air Station Pensacola in 1941. The tail stripes are willow green for an aircraft that had been assigned to the fifth section in the squadron. The P2Ys that were assigned to training duties had the former aircraft number and squadron designation over-painted and a training number assigned. (*Tailhook*)

Above: A P2Y-2, aircraft No. 28, shares the ramp with a Naval Aircraft Factory N3N trainer and a North American SNJ at Naval Air Station Pensacola in 1941. The P2Y was formerly assigned as the second aircraft in the section of a Patrol Wing 1 squadron. The lower right wing insignia has been removed because of a Bureau of Aeronautics directive. (*Tailhook*)

Right: A former Patrol Squadron 13 (VP-13) P2Y-2 is prepared for mooring at Naval Air Station Pensacola in 1941. Aircraft No. 33 was formerly assigned to Patrol Wing 1. The upper wing is painted chrome yellow, and the tail stripe is willow green. All other markings are gloss black. This P2Y-2 has the upgraded Wright R-1820-90 twin-row radials. (*Tailhook*)

Below: A black-tailed P2Y-3 (BuNo A 9569) from Patrol Squadron 7 (VP-7) makes a flight over Hawaii in the late 1930s. The cowlings and the command stripe are insignia red. A directional radio loop antenna has been added to the upper fuselage just forward of the gun positions below the upper wing. (*Tailhook*)

13

Above: A P2Y-3 from Patrol Squadron 4 (VP-4), aircraft 4-P-1, flies out over the Atlantic Ocean in the 1930s. The cowlings and commander fuselage stripe are insignia red, and the rudders are true blue. The squadron badge and engineering "E" is painted on the forward fuselage. The upper wing top is painted chrome yellow. (*Tailhook*)

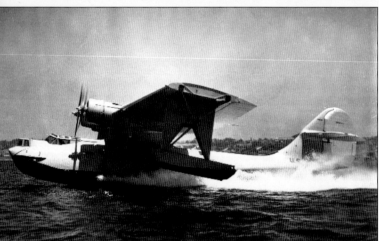

Left: The prototype XP3Y-1 Catalina (BuNo 9459) makes a takeoff run on 15 May 1936. The Catalina has the last rudder design that would be a feature of most all of the flying boat's production. The XP3Y-1 (Consolidated Model 28) was constructed at Buffalo, New York, disassembled, and taken by rail to Norfolk, Virginia, where it was reassembled for flight tests at Anacostia and Norfolk. (*Tailhook*)

Below: The XP3Y-1 prototype with an early-style rudder (second design) sits at Coco Solo, Panama Canal Zone, on 10 October 1935. One of the crew members watches from the left waist-gun position as the beaching crewmen in the water prepare to moor the new flying boat. The XP3Y-1 design was so different that a patent was granted to Consolidated Aircraft. The all-metal aircraft featured a parasol wing and retractable wingtip floats. (*Real War Photos*)

Above: The prototype XP3Y-1, now designated XPBY-1 for patrol bomber Consolidated, flies over Lindbergh Field, San Diego, California, in 1935. The XPBY-1 features the final tail design. The XPBY-1 would enter squadron service with Patrol Squadron 11F (VP-11F) in 1936. The XPBY-1 was painted overall in aluminum dope, with the top of the wing chrome yellow and the lower fuselage in a noncorrosive black. (*Tailhook*)

Right: Patrol Squadron 11 (VP-11) was the first U.S. Navy squadron to receive the PBY-2 at San Diego, California, in 1937. Aircraft 11-P-9 was the third aircraft in the third section of VP-11 and had the lower lip of cowling painted true blue. The aircraft is finished in an overall aluminum dope with chrome yellow wing tops. (*Tailhook*)

Below: A factory-fresh PBY-2 is parked for a completion photo at the Consolidated plant at Lindbergh Field, San Diego, California, on 15 May 1937. It was standard practice for the manufacturer to apply squadron markings to the aircraft. PBY-2 11-P-12 was the last aircraft assigned to VP-11. VP-11 became VP-7 in 1939 and was assigned to Patrol Wing 4. (*Consolidated Aircraft*)

Above: A PBY-4 from Patrol Squadron 13 (VP-13) makes a flight out over the Pacific in 1939. The aircraft carries the squadron code of 13-P-15 on the fuselage and aircraft number 12 on the upper wing, a carryover from when VP-13 was established at Naval Air Station San Diego in 1937 as Patrol Squadron 18 and redesignated in 1939. The center section, chevrons, and lower cowl lip are black. (*Tailhook*)

Left: An ordnanceman on a portable stand on the underwing of a PBY-2 Catalina stationed at Naval Air Station Jacksonville secures a 500-pound bomb on the rack as the two ordnancemen on the wingtop winch up the bomb. Aircraft 64 carries the neutrality star on the nose, dating the time frame to 1941. The Catalina could carry four 500-pound bombs or two 2,000-pound aerial torpedoes. (*Tailhook*)

Below: The U.S. Coast Guard purchased the second production PBY-5 (BuNo 2290) and assigned it the serial number of V189. V189 is seen over Naval Air Station San Diego in 1939. V189 was used by the U.S. Coast Guard to map the Gulf and Atlantic coasts until the start of World War II. The aircraft is finished in overall aluminum dope with chrome yellow wing tops with a black center section. The rudder is painted in red and white stripes topped by blue. (*Tailhook*)

Above: Bo-Bo, a PBY-5 serving in the Pacific, has its Pratt & Whitney R-1830-82 looked after in 1944. Consolidated provided removable work stands for the Catalina so the maintenance crews could work over land as well as water. The propellers used on the Catalina were the Hamilton-Standard Hydromatic type that gave the PBY-5 a top speed of 200 mph. (*Tailhook*)

Right: The beaching crew has removed the beaching gear from a Naval Air Station Jacksonville PBY-5 (J1-P-32), and a crewman is pulling in the restraining line. The PBY-5 is equipped with Yagi homing transmitter radar antenna arrays on both underwings. (*Tailhook*)

Below: A PBY-5 from Naval Air Station Jacksonville Training Command makes a flight over the Atlantic Ocean in 1943. A fuel dump line is fitted inboard of the aft wing strut on this aircraft. J1-P-17 does not carry any armament, as these aircraft were used only to train pilots, crew, and electronics (radar) operators. The PBY-5 has Yagi radar antennas under both wings. (*Tailhook*)

A PBY-5 is on the step and will soon be airborne. The wingtip floats will be retracted when the aircraft leaves the water. The PBYs were not fitted with flaps, as the large wing area and low wing loading made for a low takeoff and landing speed. The PBY-5 had a maximum speed of 200 mph and a maximum range of 1,965 miles. (*Tailhook*)

A PBY-5 from Patrol Squadron 23 (VP-23) sits on its beaching gear on an island in the Pacific in 1943. The aircraft is armed with four 325-pound depth bombs on the underwings. The PBY-5 is also fitted with homing radar antennas on the wing and transmitting radar antennas on the fuselage. Aircraft 23-P-80 was used as a night bomber, and it would soon be painted in an overall black scheme, earning VP-23 the name Black Cats. (*Tailhook*)

Above: A PBY-5 is launched from the seaplane ramp at Naval Air Station Corpus Christi, Texas, in 1943. The aircraft is camouflaged in the NS blue-gray over NS light gray scheme. The Catalina is still tethered to the tractor that was used for launching and recovery. Another PBY-5 is taxiing along the jetty that separated the launching area from the Gulf of Mexico. (*Tailhook*)

Right: The flight line at Naval Air Station Jacksonville, Florida, is covered with PBYs in various color schemes. J1-P-30 is camouflaged in the tri-tone scheme that was authorized in 1943. Many of the other PBYs have yellow panels on their upper wings, indicating they are trainers. Naval Air Station Jacksonville Training Command was responsible for training patrol bomber pilots and crew. (*Tailhook*)

Below: A Naval Air Station Pensacola-based PBY-5 trainer waits behind a Naval Aircraft Factory N3N floatplane trainer, called the Yellow Peril by aviation cadets, to make its takeoff run. The flight engineer of the PBY (aircraft No. 91) is standing outside the upper wing hatch. Naval Air Stations Pensacola, Jacksonville, and Corpus Christi were chosen as training bases because of their usually good flying weather. (*Tailhook*)

Above: The last production PBY-4 (BuNo 1245) was used as a test bed and designated XPBY-5A, having tricycle landing gear installed. The landing gear was uninstalled, saving 2,300 pounds, and the aircraft was converted to a PBY-R by installing windows and seats. Once converted, the PBY-5R was named Sea Mare and used to transport important personnel. The PBY-5R was finished in an overall aluminum dope with a black lower hull. (*Real War Photos*)

Left: A PBY-5A with an "eyeball turret" is hoisted aboard the seaplane tender USS *St. George* (AV-16) to undergo an engine change in May 1945. The eyeball turret contained a pair of .30-caliber machine guns in an enclosed turret. The deck of the *St. George* is littered with boxes and two crates for the Pratt & Whitney R-1830-82 engines. (*Real War Photos*)

Below: A PBY-5A from Patrol Squadron 94 (VP-94) shares the Naval Air Station Norfolk, Virginia, ramp with Naval Aircraft Factory SBN-1 from Torpedo Squadron 8 (VT-8) in early 1942. The PBY-5A, 94-P-5, is camouflaged in NS blue-gray over NS light gray with red and white rudder stripes and a red disc in the center of the national insignia. (*Real War Photos*)

Above: An early PBY-5A flies with its landing gear and wingtip floats deployed, perhaps practicing "down and dirty" stalls. The aircraft is fitted with Yagi homing antennas on the lower wing and transmitting antennas on the forward fuselage sides. The small stub at the upper wingtip is for the high-frequency wire antenna. (*Tailhook*)

Right: A PBY-5A makes a practice approach at altitude, determining the stall speeds with the gear and floats extended. This function would be tested with the aircraft at various weights and altitudes to determine performance. When the PBY-5A was introduced in 1940, the versatility of the Catalina was greatly increased. Boeing of Canada also constructed the PBY-5A. (*Tailhook*)

Below: A PBY-5A, probably from Patrol Squadron 43, makes a landing on a very muddy Aleutian landing strip in Alaska in March 1942. The Dodge ambulance has been called to attend to the pilot of the Curtiss P-40 Tomahawk that has crashed and left the runway. Operating conditions during the spring thaw were less than conducive to aircraft operations. (*Tailhook*)

Above: A PBY-5A flies over the rugged snow-covered coast of Alaska in 1943. The American armed forces had to retake a part of the Aleutian island chain after the Japanese attacked in 1942. The flying conditions in the Alaska region presented a continuous problem for aviators, summer or winter. (*Tailhook*)

Left: A PBY-5A taxis up to the beach at Sand Point, Shumagin Islands, Alaska, in 1942. The aircraft director, with raised arms, will direct the Catalina to a spot on the beach. The PBY-5A is camouflaged in the NS blue-gray over NS light gray with oversize national insignias on the wings and fuselage. The rudder stripes are red and white. The derrick in the background is a pile driver that would be used to construct a pier. (*Real War Photos*)

Below: A PBY-5A is getting the left Pratt & Whitney R-1830-82 engine attended to. The PBY-5A, No. 27, is camouflaged in the Atlantic Scheme No. II of NS gull gray over white. The PBY-5A off the right wingtip is camouflaged in the NS blue-gray over NS light gray with a yellow surround on the national insignia. The yellow surround was used during "Operation Torch," the Invasion of North Africa and Sicily. (*Tailhook*)

The ramp at Narsarssuak, Greenland, is host to U.S. Coast Guard PBY-5A Catalinas from Patrol Squadron 6CG (VP-6CG), the only patrol squadron manned solely by U.S. Coast Guard airmen. The Narsarssuak base was established in 1943 and given the code name Blue West One (BW-1), and the PBY-5As were used for convoy protection and anti-submarine duties. (*USCG*)

A PBY-5A Catalina flies along the rugged coast of Alaska in 1943. Aircraft No. 51, probably from VP-43, is equipped with Yagi radar antennas under the wing and additional high-frequency wire antennas strung from the pylon to the vertical stabilizer. The four vertical items between the engine nacelles are fuel tank vents. (*Tailhook*)

Above: A parachute-dropped AR-8 rescue boat is being winched up under the right wing of a U.S. Coast Guard PBY-6A at the Naval Air Test Center, Patuxent River, Maryland, in 1946. The boat would be dropped to survivors of torpedoed ships and downed aircraft when sea conditions precluded the landing of the aircraft. (*USCG*)

Left: A U.S. Coast Guard PBY-5A operating in the air-sea rescue role shares the ramp with a North American SNJ trainer, a pair of Beech JRB utility transports, and a few PBY-5A Catalinas immediately after World War II. The aircraft has yellow wingtips, floats, center section of the wing, and fuselage stripe, all banded in black. (*USCG*)

Below: A U.S. Coast Guard PBY-5A (BuNo 433939) sits on the ramp still carrying the SR-2c scheme authorized in 1943, which called for all horizontal surfaces to be painted a gloss sea blue and all undersurfaces to be painted a gloss white. Aircraft ARS-485 has yellow wing panels and fuselage stripe and international orange tail and wing panels, all banded with black. (*USCG*)

Above: A U.S. Naval Reserve PBY-6A sits on beaching gear, perhaps due to a landing gear malfunction. Aircraft 203 V has the eyeball turret and covers over the exhaust for the deicing wing boots. The aircraft is camouflaged in an overall gloss Navy blue with an orange-yellow fuselage band and panel under the nose. (*Tailhook*)

Right: An early PBY-6A is camouflaged in an overall scheme of gloss Navy blue. The nose of the radome is in a light beige, and the propeller-warning stripe is red. The right cowling has gloss white on the lower side, indicating that it was taken off another aircraft. The main gear wheel has been left in the natural aluminum finish. (*Tailhook*)

Below: The prototype Model 31 was rolled out of the Consolidated plant at San Diego, California, in 1939. The Model 31 was constructed in secret as a private venture to sell to the U.S. Navy. The Model 31 was painted in an overall aluminum dope finish with black hull and carries the civilian registration of NX-21731. The civilian registration, "Consolidated Aircraft Corp.," and "Model 31" have been painted in black on the vertical stabilizers. (*SAM*)

Above: The Model 31 made its first flight on 5 May 1939 from Lindbergh Field, and it was soon discovered that the Model 31 had a top speed of almost 250 mph. The Model 31 used the Davis wing and a pair of Wright 2,000-horsepower R-3350 twin-row radial engines. The Consolidated employees dubbed the Model 31 The Whale. (*SAM*)

Left: The Model 31 flies out over the Consolidated factory in 1939. The aircraft featured retractable wing floats and twin slab vertical stabilizers. The 4,000-pound bomb load, (eight 500-pound bombs or two 2,000-pound torpedoes) was to be carried internally. Even with the Model 31's impressive speed and range of 2,300 miles, the U.S. Navy still was not interested in purchasing the aircraft. (*SAM*)

Below: In April 1942, the U.S. Navy purchased the Model 31 and designated the aircraft the XP4Y-1, giving it the bureau number 27852. The XP4Y-1 had the tail raised, and dummy turrets were installed. A dummy 37 mm cannon and radome were installed in the nose. The aircraft was camouflaged in the NS blue-gray over NS light gray scheme. The XP4Y-1 was officially named the Corregidor in 1942. (*SAM*)

Above: The XP4Y-1 has had its beaching gear removed, although the gear could be retracted into the fuselage, for a test flight in 1942. The wing floats retracted inward instead of outward as on the PBY Catalina series. The aircraft would be tethered by the wing floats until the pilot gave the signal to remove them. (*SAM*)

Right: The XP4Y-1 was to go into production at a new factory constructed in New Orleans, Louisiana, but the entire production of the Wright R-3350 engines was diverted to the Boeing B-29. The contract for XP4Y-1 was cancelled, and the New Orleans factory was awarded a contract to build 450 Catalinas. (*SAM*)

Below: The prototype XPB2Y-1 (BuNo 0453) is photographed outside the Consolidated factory on 7 December 1937. The aircraft was assembled with a single vertical stabilizer like the Sikorsky XPBS-1, both of which were constructed to a U.S. Navy request for proposal for a four-engine patrol bomber. The XPB4Y-1 sits on removable beaching gear. (*Tailhook*)

Above: Flight-testing revealed a lack of stability, and a pair of twin vertical stabilizers was installed on the XPB2Y-1 in place of the single stabilizer to correct the directional control problems. The aircraft was painted in an overall aluminum dope scheme with a chrome yellow wing top. The bottom of the retractable wingtip floats and the hull bottom is painted in a noncorrosive black. (*Tailhook*)

Left: The large nose turret on the XPB2Y-1 was designed to house a single .50-caliber manually operated machine gun. The tail turret would also be equipped with a single .50-caliber machine gun. Since this was a test/prototype aircraft, no weapons were installed. The 4,000-pound bomb load was housed in bays in the inner wings. (*Tailhook*)

Below: The XPB2Y-1 was assigned to the commander of the Aircraft Scouting Force, Pacific, in 1940, making it the first flag plane. The XPB2Y-1 has been armed with a single .50-caliber machine gun in the tail turret. The XPB2Y-1 had a maximum speed of 250 mph and a range of 4,320 miles. The black stripe running along the hull was called a "boot topping," and its purpose was the same as it is on ships, to prevent fouling. (*Tailhook*)

Above: An underside view shows the XPB2Y-1 being used by the commander of the Aircraft Scouting Force, Pacific. Four Pratt & Whitney XR-1830-72 radials that developed 1,050 horsepower for takeoff powered the aircraft. In 1942, the aircraft was assigned to Patrol Squadron 13 (VP-13), a unit that would be used to train future PB2Y pilots and crew. (*Tailhook*)

Right: A PB2Y-2 (BuNo 1633), the first production aircraft, was assigned to the commander of VP-13 in 1941. VP-13 operated as the Transitional Training Unit, Pacific. This craft, 13-P-1, has a red stripe on the vertical stabilizers, a red fuselage band, and red cowlings. The propellers have black spinners. A neutrality star has been painted on the nose for recognition. The hull has a modified shape, and a newly designed nose turret has been installed. (*Tailhook*)

Below: A PB2Y-3R (BuNo 7235) was a PB2Y-3 that was converted to a transport by removing all gun turrets, fairing them over, and adding a large cargo door. Provisions were made to accommodate 44 passengers. The engines were changed to R-1830-92s with the inner engines driving a four-blade prop and the outer engines a three-blade prop. The Naval Air Transport Service (NATS) badge is painted on the nose. (*Tailhook*)

A PB2Y-3R (BuNo 7152) makes a takeoff run in 1943 following conversion from PB2Y-3 standards. A pitot tube extends out of the cockpit roof. The PB2Y-3R still is equipped with the R-1830-88 radial engines with three-blade props. Once airborne, the wingtip floats and the flaps would be retracted. (*U.S. Navy*)

The last production PB2Y-2 (BuNo 1638) sits on beaching gear at the Consolidated seaplane ramp at San Diego, California. The aircraft was converted in 1942 to an XPB2Y-3 and then to an XPB2Y-5 with an engine change to R-1830-92 engines with four-blade props. Many of the PB2Y-3s that were not converted to transports were converted to PB2Y-5s. (*Tailhook*)

Above: Contract Operation, a PB2Y-3R (BuNo 7078), taxis in the harbor at Naval Air Station Hilo, Territory of Hawaii, in 1945. The aircraft is camouflaged in the tri-tone scheme that was authorized in 1943, and a NATS badge is on the nose. The flight crew has opened the cockpit roof escape hatches to allow some cool air into the cockpit. (*National Archives*)

Right: A PB2Y-3R (BuNo 7230) is camouflaged in an overall gloss Navy blue scheme. The aircraft is fitted with a pair of football-shaped direction-finder antennas. The aircraft commander has his sliding side cockpit window opened to add some cool air to the all-glass cockpit. The obligatory NATS badge has been added below the cockpit. (*Tailhook*)

Below: A PB2Y-5 from Patrol Bombing Squadron 15 (VPB-15) makes a patrol flight in 1944. The PB2Y-5 was armed with six .50-caliber machine guns, two each in the nose, dorsal, and tail powered turrets. The PB2Y-5 is camouflaged in the tri-tone scheme. A dorsal search antenna has been placed atop the fuselage between the wing root and cockpit area. (*Tailhook*)

Above: A PB2Y-5 (BuNo 7179), R51, a converted PB2Y-3, flies over Hawaii in 1945. R-1830-92 engines with four-blade props powered the PB2Y-5. All of the PB2Y-5 patrol bombers had the search radar mounted atop the forward fuselage. This PB2Y-5 was camouflaged in the tri-tone scheme. (*Tailhook*)

Left: Consolidated PB2Y-5H was equipped as a flying hospital by installing the capability to carry litters. The aircraft is still fitted with power-operated nose and tail turrets for self-defense. The PB2Y-5H has an unusual application of the tri-tone scheme. The -5H is also equipped with four-blade props on the inboard engines and three-blade props on the outboard engines. (*Tailhook*)

Below: Five PB2Y-5-H/Rs from a transport squadron fly in formation in 1945. The nearest aircraft, X60 (BuNo 7061), has the side cargo door open. The PB2Y-5-H/R is equipped with R-1830-92 radial engines and the search radar atop the fuselage. (*Tailhook*)

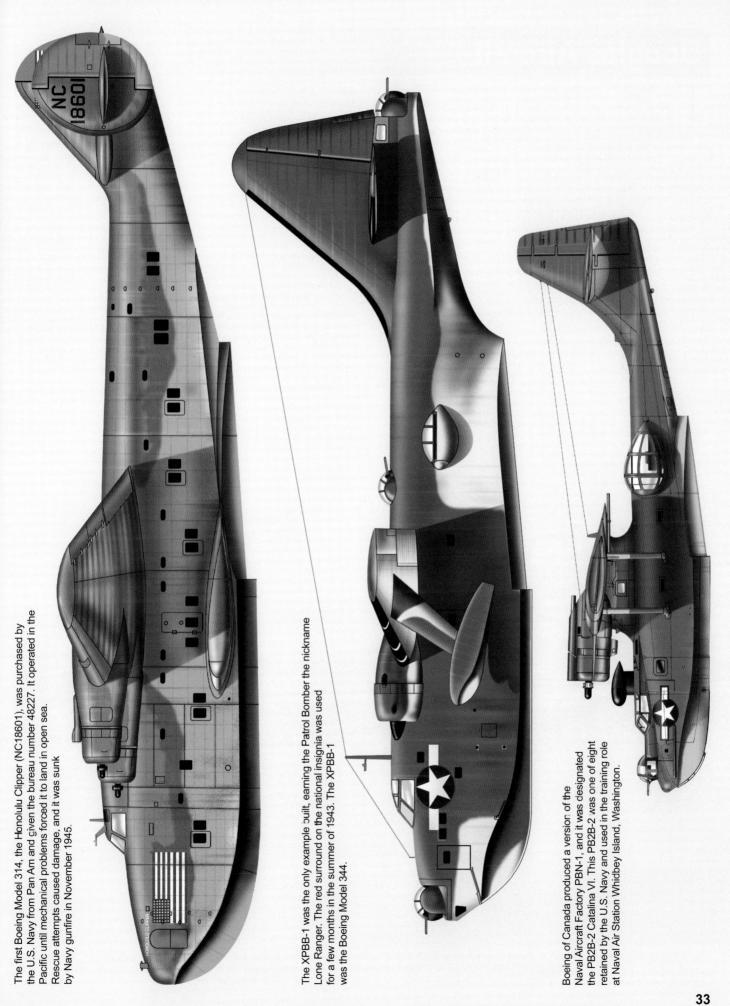

The first Boeing Model 314, the Honolulu Clipper (NC18601), was purchased by the U.S. Navy from Pan Am and given the bureau number 48227. It operated in the Pacific until mechanical problems forced it to land in open sea. Rescue attempts caused damage, and it was sunk by Navy gunfire in November 1945.

The XPBB-1 was the only example built, earning the Patrol Bomber the nickname Lone Ranger. The red surround on the national insignia was used for a few months in the summer of 1943. The XPBB-1 was the Boeing Model 344.

Boeing of Canada produced a version of the Naval Aircraft Factory PBN-1, and it was designated the PB2B-2 Catalina VI. This PB2B-2 was one of eight retained by the U.S. Navy and used in the training role at Naval Air Station Whidbey Island, Washington.

33

Douglas Aircraft

The Douglas Aircraft Co. was founded by Donald W. Douglas in Santa Monica, California, in 1921. Douglas had worked for Glenn L. Martin Aircraft before helping to form Davis-Douglas Co. When Davis-Douglas Co. ceased to exist, Douglas formed the Douglas Aircraft Co. The Douglas Aircraft Co. began producing the DT-1 and DT-2 single-engine and the T2D twin-engine torpedo bombers for the U.S. Navy in 1921.

In 1924, four specially built Douglas World Cruisers (DWC) set out to circle the globe. The DWCs were modified versions of the DT-2 torpedo bomber. The flight took 175 days, and only two aircraft were able to complete the trip; one crashed in Alaska, and the other had mechanical failure.

Douglas would build one flying boat that was used during World War II, the RD series of flying boats called the Sinbad or Dolphin. In 1931, the U.S. Navy and the U.S. Coast Guard ordered the RD. The RD-series craft were not amphibians; although the main landing gear retracted, it was not strong enough to support the aircraft for a landing on a runway.

The XRD-1 was designated as a transport, thus the "X" for experimental, "R" for transport, and "D" for Douglas Aircraft. The aircraft was used basically for search-and-rescue missions. The U.S. Coast Guard ordered 13 RDs in four different series — an RD, an RD-1, an RD-2, and 10 RD-4s. During their service with the Coast Guard, three were lost to accidents and five survived to serve in World War II. The rest were decommissioned and replaced by Grumman amphibians at various air stations around the United States.

The U.S. Navy ordered the XRD-1 (BuNo A-8876) for evaluation. The XRD-1 was powered by a pair of Pratt & Whitney R-985 Wasp Junior radial engines that were fitted above the wing on struts, and the aircraft were fitted with eight seats. Three of the RD-2s were purchased by the Navy, and one went to the U.S. Marine Corps. The last Navy purchase was for six RD-3s, basically RD-2s but powered by a pair of Pratt & Whitney R-1340-96 radials with 450 horsepower each. Two of the RD-3s went to the Marines. The RD-4 was the Coast Guard version of the Navy RD-3.

Douglas received a contract in 1933 from the U.S. Navy to construct one prototype twin-engine flying boat, designated as the XP3D-1. Consolidated also made a prototype, the XP3Y-1, later known as the PBY Catalina. Douglas lost the contract because its price was higher than that of the Consolidated entry.

Douglas would be remembered by its Douglas Commercial (DC) line of transport aircraft for the civilian and military market. The DC-3/C-47 was the most widely produced transport plane during World War II. Imitation is the sincerest form of flattery, and both Japan and Russia produced versions of the aircraft during World War II. Douglas in 1967 merged with McDonnell Aircraft, forming McDonnell Douglas. In 1997, McDonnell merged with Boeing, ending an era that spanned 75 years for the Douglas Aircraft Co.

The Douglas RD-2 served with the U.S. Coast Guard in June 1932. The aircraft was named Adhara after a star in the Canis Major constellation. The RD-2 was serving with the U.S. Coast Guard and was painted in a dark blue, with aluminum dope lower wings and hull area. The vertical stabilizer is painted, front to back, red, white, and blue. Adhara was lost in a fatal accident on 5 December 1938 while attempting a rescue. (USCG)

Above: The Douglas RD series craft were called "flying lifeboats" because they could land on water, effect a rescue, and take off. This RD-4 carried the U.S. Coast Guard serial 132 and was named Alloth after a star in the Ursa Major system. Before 1940, the aircraft was re-serialled V127 and served at San Diego, California. The landing gear was semi-retractable and could only be used for beaching the aircraft. (*USCG*)

Right: The Mizar, an RD-4 named after a star in the Ursa Major constellation, was stationed in the New York area in the 1930s. The U.S. Coast Guard serial 131 was changed before World War II to V126. This craft crashed on 5 August 1941 while flying out of Air Station San Francisco, California, while on routine patrol. (*USCG*)

Below: The Alloth, an RD-4, was originally stationed at U.S. Coast Guard Air Base Biloxi, Mississippi. The RD-4 was powered by a pair of Pratt & Whitney 454-horsepower R-1340 Wasp radial engines, giving it a maximum speed of 147 mph. The Alloth is painted overall in aluminum dope finish with yellow wing tops. The U.S. Coast Guard emblem is carried on the nose. (*USCG*)

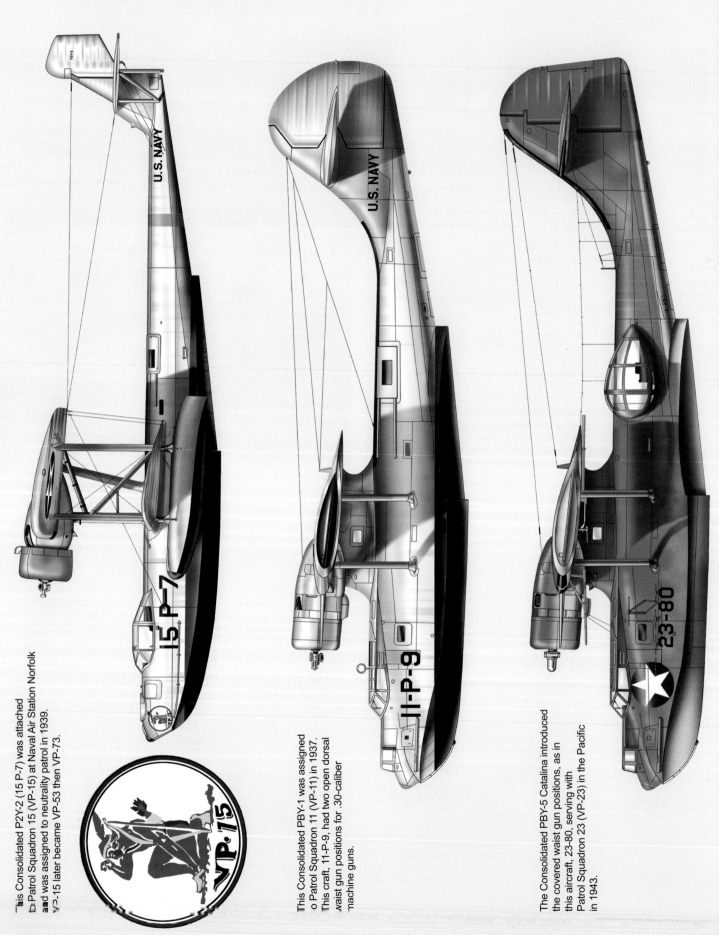

This Consolidated P2Y-2 (15 P-7) was attached
to Patrol Squadron 15 (VP-15) at Naval Air Station Norfolk
and was assigned to neutrality patrol in 1939.
VP-15 later became VP-53 then VP-73.

This Consolidated PBY-1 was assigned
to Patrol Squadron 11 (VP-11) in 1937.
This craft, 11-P-9, had two open dorsal
waist gun positions for .30-caliber
machine guns.

The Consolidated PBY-5 Catalina introduced
the covered waist gun positions, as in
this aircraft, 23-80, serving with
Patrol Squadron 23 (VP-23) in the Pacific
in 1943.

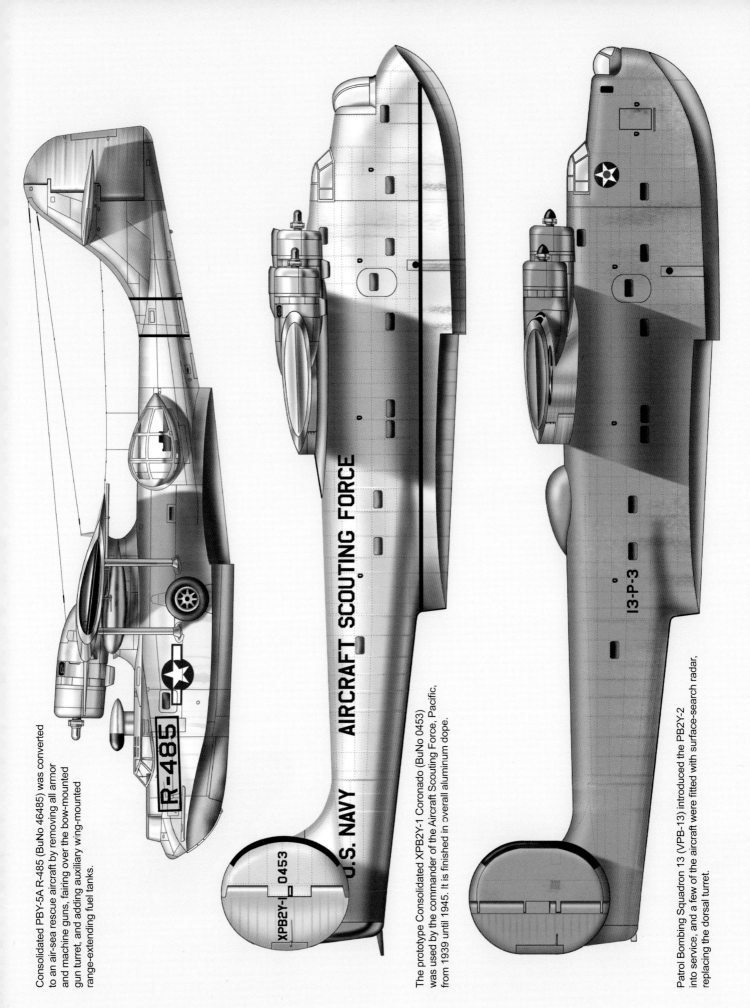

Consolidated PBY-5A R-485 (BuNo 46485) was converted to an air-sea rescue aircraft by removing all armor and machine guns, fairing over the bow-mounted gun turret, and adding auxiliary wing-mounted range-extending fuel tanks.

R-485

XPB2Y-1   0453

U.S. NAVY   AIRCRAFT SCOUTING FORCE

The prototype Consolidated XPB2Y-1 Coronado (BuNo 0453) was used by the commander of the Aircraft Scouting Force, Pacific, from 1939 until 1945. It is finished in overall aluminum dope.

13-P-3

Patrol Bombing Squadron 13 (VPB-13) introduced the PB2Y-2 into service, and a few of the aircraft were fitted with surface-search radar, replacing the dorsal turret.

When the Japanese attacked Pearl Harbor in 1941, the U.S. Coast Guard had seven operational RD-4s in its inventory. By the start of the war, all of the RD-4s were painted in an overall light gray scheme. The landing gear is in its fully retracted position. The national insignia carries the red center disc, and the tail has the red and white stripes topped by blue. (*USCG*)

A U.S. Coast Guard RD-4, named Vega after a star in the constellation Lyra, sits on the seaplane ramp at San Francisco on 3 June 1942. The national insignia has been painted oversize as an additional recognition feature. The RD-4 carring the U.S. Coast Guard serial number V128. The aircraft is camouflaged in the NS blue-gray over NS light gray scheme. (*William T. Larkins*)

The Capella, an RD-4 named for a star in the Aurida constellation, makes a flyby in the mid-1930s. The RD-4 carries the serial number 137, but that was changed to V132 before World War II. The Capella served with U.S. Coast Guard Air Base Miami, Florida, until 1943. The RD-4 has twin direction-finder loop antennas. (*USCG*)

Grumman

The Grumman Aeronautical Engineering Co. was formed in 1929 by Leroy Grumman and Leon Swirbul on Long Island, New York. The name Grumman was used because he owned the most shares. Both men had worked at Loening Aeronautical Engineering Co. and perhaps borrowed some of the name when they formed their new company. When Loening announced that it was selling its Long Island operation to Keystone Aircraft and moving to Bristol, Pennsylvania, Grumman and Swirbul quit and decided to form their own aircraft company.

Grumman built its first plane for the U.S. Navy in 1931, the portly XFF-1. The XFF-1 used a biplane layout with retractable landing gear and a Wright R-1820 radial engine that gave it a maximum speed of 195 mph. Later designs, the FF-1, F2F, and F3F, were also biplanes. When Grumman introduced the F4F Wildcat, a new era in naval aviation was born. Along with the Douglas SBD Dauntless and the Douglas TBD Devastator, the Grumman F4F Wildcat was considered one of the saviors at the Battles of the Coral Sea and Midway in 1942.

Grumman built three types of amphibians used by the U.S. Navy, U.S. Marine Corps, and U.S. Coast Guard during World War II — the JF and J2F Duck, the J4F Widgeon, and the JRF Goose. The JF and J2F were single-engine biplanes, and the JRF and J4F were twin-engine high-wing monoplanes. All had retractable landing gears.

Relying heavily on the Loening Aircraft OL series of amphibians, Grumman introduced its Model G-9, designated the XJF-1 Duck. The prototype was tested, and the U.S. Navy ordered 27 JF-1s, with one going to the U.S. Marine Corps. The Pratt & Whitney R-1830 Twin Wasp powered the JF-1 series. Fourteen JF-2s were built for the U.S. Coast Guard, and four were built for the Argentinian navy. They were powered by Wright R-1820-102 radial engines. The U.S. Coast Guard traded in four of the JF-2s for four NAF N3N Canaries, also known as the Yellow Peril. An engine change to a Wright R-1820-80 brought about the JF-3; four were built.

The J2F series was the Grumman Model 15, which had the inner aileron struts omitted and a redesigned cabin that could accommodate two passengers as well as the crew of two. Twenty-nine J2F-1s were constructed, and the Wright R-1820-20 powered the amphibians. The J2F-2 was constructed for the U.S. Navy and U.S. Marine Corps to use in the Virgin Islands. The J2F-3 was constructed for the U.S. Navy, also for use in the Virgin Islands on neutrality patrol. An engine change brought about the J2F-3. Another engine change created the J2F-4, to which target-towing gear was added. The J2F-5 was the same as the J2F-2 but with an engine change, and it was the last Duck built by Grumman. Columbia Aircraft constructed the J2F-6, as the Grumman production line was being used to produce the F6F Hellcat exclusively.

Grumman built two twin-engine amphibians for the U.S. Navy; both were derived from civilian models introduced by Grumman before World War II. The Grumman Model G-26 was the military version of the civilian Model G-21A. A single prototype XJ3F Goose was tested by the U.S. Navy and put into production as the JRF-1 Goose. The seven-seat amphibian was powered by a pair of Pratt & Whitney R-985 Wasp Junior engines, giving the Goose a maximum speed of just over 200 mph. Five JRF-1As were produced, and they had aerial survey and photographic equipment installed. The JRF-2 was a version constructed for the U.S. Coast Guard. The JRF-3 was identical to the JRF-2, but deicing boots were installed on all leading edges for use in colder climates.

The JRF-4 had provisions to carry two 250-pound bombs under the wings. The most widely produced version was the JRF-5, with 185 being produced. The JRF-6 was constructed for Lend-Lease to Great Britain. Some civilian Grumman G-21As were also pressed into U.S. Navy service.

The final Grumman amphibian produced was the J4F Widgeon, the military version of the Grumman Model G-44A. Two versions were constructed, the J4F-1 for the U.S. Coast Guard and the J4F-2 for the U.S. Navy. Both of the J4F versions were powered by a pair of air-cooled Ranger L-440 Inverted-V engines that produced 220 horsepower. The J4F-1 had provisions on the starboard wing to carry a 325-pound depth charge. Both versions could carry up to five passengers.

Grumman was perhaps better known for producing premier fighter aircraft for the U.S. Navy for more than 70 years. The Cat series of aircraft ruled the skies over the world's oceans, flying from aircraft carriers. Its last fighter, the F-14 Tomcat, served the U. S. Navy for more than 30 years before retiring from service in 2006. In 1994, Grumman was merged into Northrop, creating the Northrop Grumman Corp.

The first production Grumman JF-1 (BuNo 9434) was assigned to Utility Squadron 1 (VJ-1). It was assigned as the third aircraft in the section and given the aircraft code of 1-J-3. The tail and vertical stabilizer were painted willow green. The JF-1 owed its float and fuselage design to the Loening OL-5 amphibian. The JF-1 was called Duck because, like the feathered version, it could operate from water or land. (*Tailhook*)

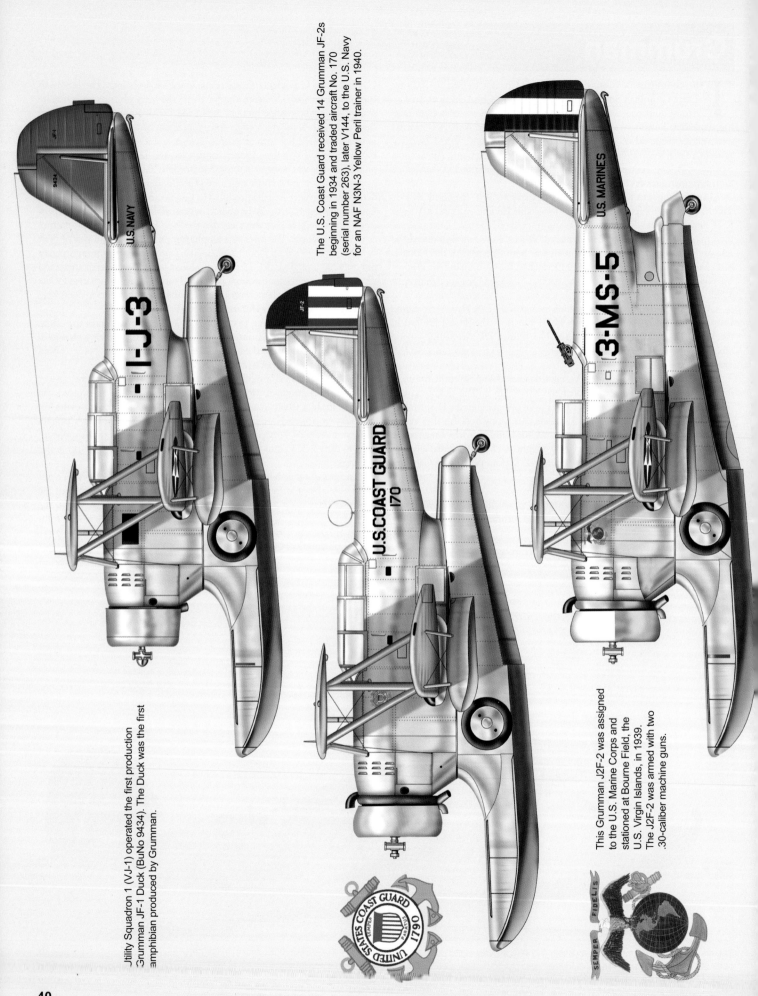

Utility Squadron 1 (VJ-1) operated the first production Grumman JF-1 Duck (BuNo 9434). The Duck was the first amphibian produced by Grumman.

The U.S. Coast Guard received 14 Grumman JF-2s beginning in 1934 and traded aircraft No. 170 (serial number 263), later V144, to the U.S. Navy for an NAF N3N-3 Yellow Peril trainer in 1940.

This Grumman J2F-2 was assigned to the U.S. Marine Corps and stationed at Bourne Field, the U.S. Virgin Islands, in 1939. The J2F-2 was armed with two .30-caliber machine guns.

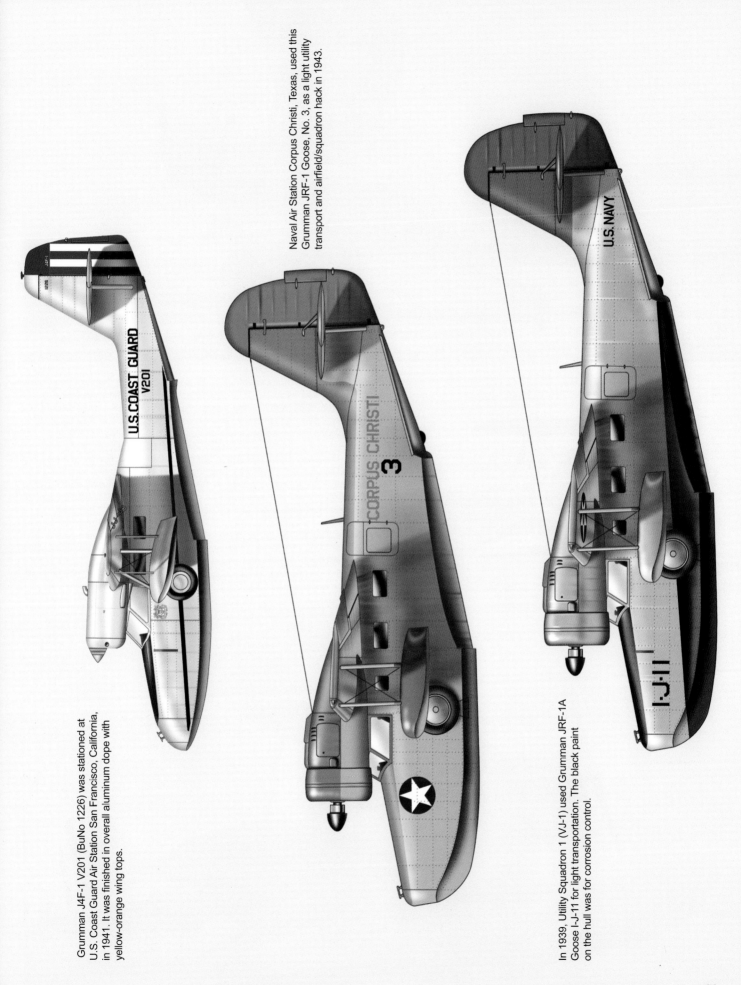

Grumman J4F-1 V201 (BuNo 1226) was stationed at U.S. Coast Guard Air Station San Francisco, California, in 1941. It was finished in overall aluminum dope with yellow-orange wing tops.

Naval Air Station Corpus Christi, Texas, used this Grumman JRF-1 Goose, No. 3, as a light utility transport and airfield/squadron hack in 1943.

In 1939, Utility Squadron 1 (VJ-1) used Grumman JRF-1A Goose I-J-11 for light transportation. The black paint on the hull was for corrosion control.

Above: The third production JF-1 (BuNo 9436) sits on the Grumman ramp before it was assigned to a squadron. The JF-1 is finished overall in an aluminum dope with chrome-yellow wing tops. The JF-1 was used in the scouting, search-and-rescue, and photographic roles. The national insignia was placed in four positions, with no insignia on the fuselage. (*Tailhook*)

Left: This JF-1 (BuNo 9440) was assigned to the USS *Ranger* (CV-4) utility squadron in 1940. The JF-1 was the No. 6 aircraft in the squadron. The aircraft is camouflaged overall in the NS light gray that was authorized in December 1940. The arresting hook added versatility and enabled the aircraft to operate off land, water, and the deck of an aircraft carrier. (*Tailhook*)

Below: The No. 5 aircraft in the USS *Ranger*'s utility squadron was a JF-1 (BuNo 9439). A Pratt & Whitney 700-horsepower R-1830-62 radial engine powered the JF-1, giving the aircraft a maximum speed of 168 mph and a service ceiling of 18,000 feet. The fuselage and float were constructed of aluminum, and the wings and all flying surfaces were fabric-covered. (*Tailhook*)

Above: A Pratt & Whitney R-1830-62 radial engine powered the first Grumman JF-2 procured by the U.S. Coast Guard. A Wright Cyclone radial powered subsequent JF-2s. Aircraft 161 was eventually reserialled as V161. The JF-2 is fitted with a tail wheel that was used on the arrestor hook-equipped JF-1 models. This JF-2 crashed off Cape May, New Jersey, on 19 January 1935, killing the pilot. (*Tailhook*)

Right: A U.S. Marine Corps J2F-1 Duck serves with Marine Scouting Squadron 2 (VMS-2) at Naval Air Station San Diego, California, in 1939. The panel covering the blower housing has been removed for maintenance. The U.S. Marine Corps emblem and a suction venturi for the aircraft instruments are placed at the wing cabane area. The float on the J2F-1 was extended one foot forward to improve water performance. (*Tailhook*)

Below: A Grumman J2F-1 serves with the USS *Lexington* (CV-2) utility squadron in 1941. The aircraft is camouflaged in an overall light gray scheme adopted in December 1940. "USS Lexington" and the aircraft number, "4," are painted in white. The aircraft is not equipped with an arresting hook. (*Tailhook*)

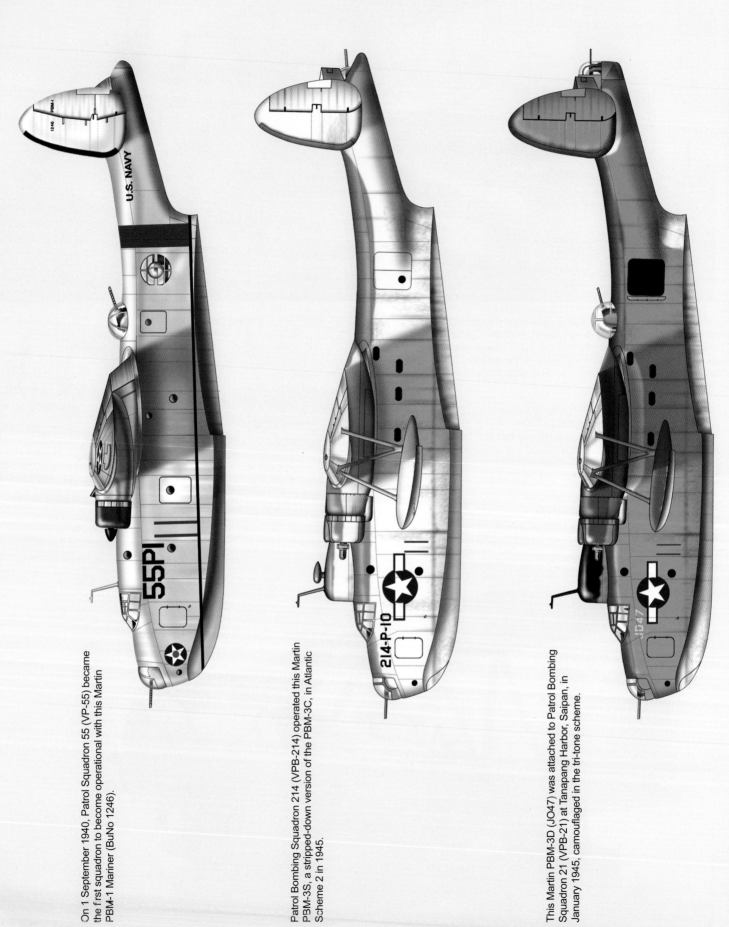

On 1 September 1940, Patrol Squadron 55 (VP-55) became the first squadron to become operational with this Martin PBM-1 Mariner (BuNo 1246).

Patrol Bombing Squadron 214 (VPB-214) operated this Martin PBM-3S, a stripped-down version of the PBM-3C, in Atlantic Scheme 2 in 1945.

This Martin PBM-3D (JO47) was attached to Patrol Bombing Squadron 21 (VPB-21) at Tanapang Harbor, Saipan, in January 1945, camouflaged in the tri-tone scheme.

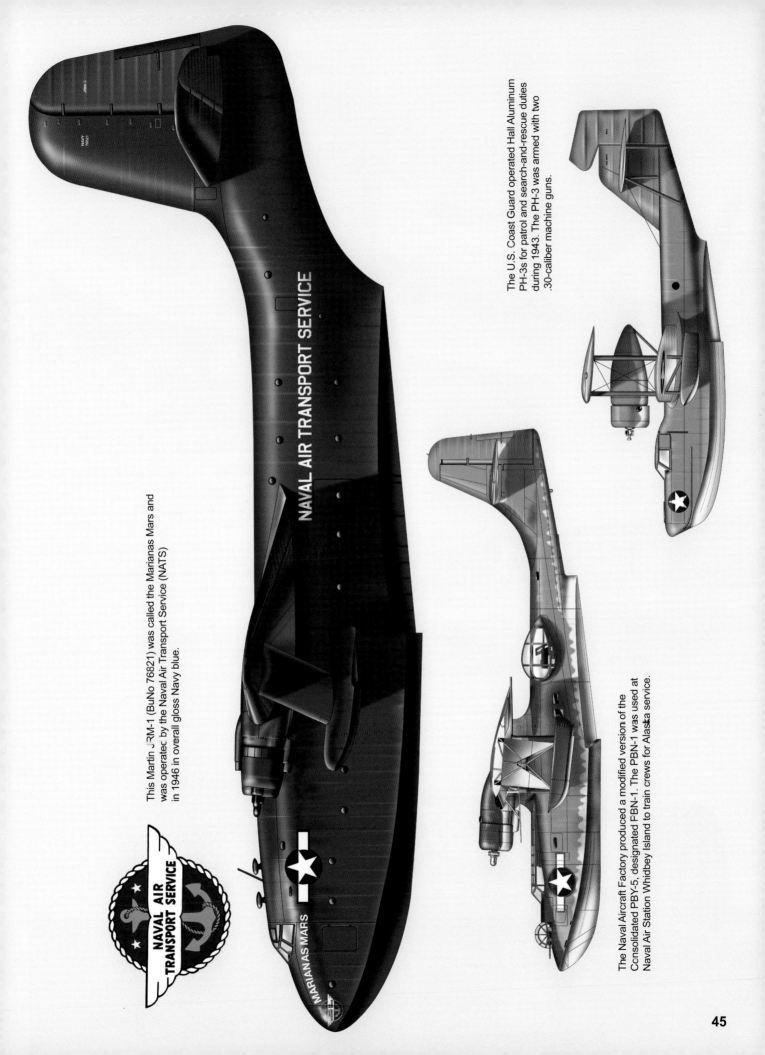

This Martin JRM-1 (BuNo 76821) was called the Marianas Mars and was operated by the Naval Air Transport Service (NATS) in 1946 in overall gloss Navy blue.

The U.S. Coast Guard operated Hall Aluminum PH-3s for patrol and search-and-rescue duties during 1943. The PH-3 was armed with two .30-caliber machine guns.

The Naval Aircraft Factory produced a modified version of the Consolidated PBY-5, designated PBN-1. The PBN-1 was used at Naval Air Station Whidbey Island to train crews for Alaska service.

Above: A JF-1 (BuNo 9442) was assigned as aircraft number 5 to the USS *Lexington* (CV-2) utility squadron in 1939. The aircraft is finished overall in a NS light gray scheme with blue, white, and red rudder stripes. The crew has boarded the aircraft to fly out to the carrier for an arrested landing. The Grumman JF-1 would serve with the U.S. Navy until 1955. (*Tailhook*)

Left: The U.S. Coast Guard acquired 14 Grumman JF-2s, with the first being received in 1934. A Wright Cyclone 775-horsepower R-1820-102 radial engine driving a 9-foot-diameter three-blade Hamilton Standard prop powered the JF-2. This gave the JF-2 a maximum speed of 176 mph and a service ceiling of 18,500 feet. (*USCG*)

Below: An overall aluminum dope, with orange-yellow wing tops, JF-2 (serial number 170) sits on a grass ramp in 1935. The serial would be changed to V144 before the war. A loop direction-finder antenna is situated on the fuselage spine just behind the radio operator/observer's cockpit. The square window below the observer's cockpit is for a third crewman. (*Tailhook*)

Above: The utility squadron from USS *Saratoga* (CV-3) flew this arrestor hook-equipped J2F-1 in 1941. The aircraft is camouflaged overall in a light gray scheme with "USS *Saratoga*" and the assigned aircraft number, "5," painted in white. The aircraft has been fitted with a trailing wire antenna for the high-frequency radio. The wire antenna could also be used as a "hard" altimeter. (*Tailhook*)

Right: This Grumman JF-2 served with the U.S. Coast Guard at Air Station Port Angeles, Washington. In January 1941, V144 was traded to the U.S. Navy and assigned the bureau number 00372. The U.S. Coast Guard serial number V144 is painted on the fuselage side as well as on the bottom of the float. A football-shaped direction-finder antenna has been placed on the fuselage spine. (*USCG*)

Below: The first production J2F-1 (BuNo 0162) was used at Naval Air Station Anacostia, Maryland, Naval Air Test Center to test the full-span upper wing flaps. The aircraft is finished in an overall aluminum dope with yellow wing tops. "Anacostia," "U.S. Navy," "0162," and "J2F-1" are painted in black. Additional coverings have been placed over the third crewman compartment windows. (*Tailhook*)

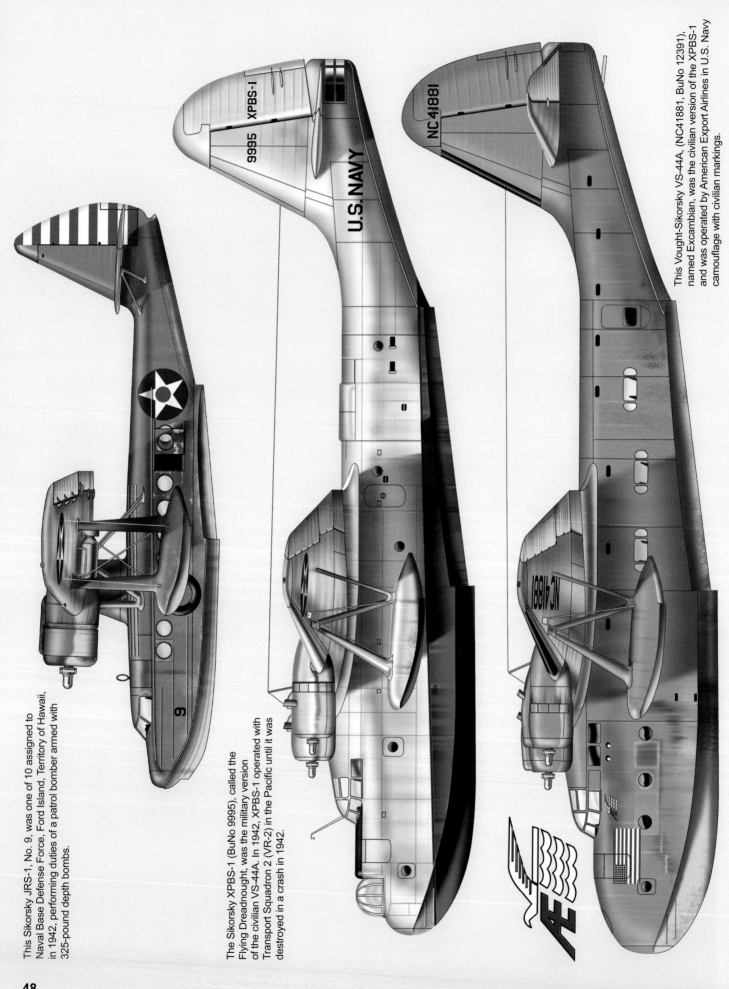

This Sikorsky JRS-1, No. 9, was one of 10 assigned to Naval Base Defense Force, Ford Island, Territory of Hawaii, in 1942, performing duties of a patrol bomber armed with 325-pound depth bombs.

The Sikorsky XPBS-1 (BuNo 9995), called the Flying Dreadnought, was the military version of the civilian VS-44A. In 1942, XPBS-1 operated with Transport Squadron 2 (VR-2) in the Pacific until it was destroyed in a crash in 1942.

This Vought-Sikorsky VS-44A, (NC41881, BuNo 12391), named Excambian, was the civilian version of the XPBS-1 and was operated by American Export Airlines in U.S. Navy camouflage with civilian markings.

Above: A J2F-1 (BuNo 0189) from Fleet Air Base Hawaii flies out over the Pacific in 1939. The Fleet Air Base was located on Ford Island in Pearl Harbor. Aircraft No. 9 is finished in an overall aluminum dope with yellow wing tops. This J2F-1 is not equipped with an arrestor hook but has provisions for one to be mounted. (*Tailhook*)

Right: A J2F-4 from Utility Squadron 3 (VJ-3), 3-J-24, flies over the clouds in 1940. The aircraft is finished in an overall aluminum dope scheme with yellow wing tops and white vertical and horizontal stabilizers. VJ-3 operated out of Puunene Airfield, Hawaii, towing targets and serving as a general utility transport for the fleet. (*Tailhook*)

Below: A J2F-2 from Fleet Photographic Reconnaissance Squadron 2 (VD-2), Atlantic, engages in a rescue at sea simulation in 1943. The pilot, without shoes, is being assisted into the rubber raft by the observer as the third crewman holds the tiny raft. VD-2 operated out of Norfolk, Virginia, performing equipment testing and other duties by the direct orders of the Bureau of Aeronautics. (*Tailhook*)

Above: A U.S. Marine Corps Grumman J2F-2 serving with Marine Utility Squadron 3 (VMS-3) sits beached on the sand at Charlotte Amalie, St. Thomas, Virgin Islands, in 1940. The J2F-2 has a single .30-caliber machine gun in the observer's position and bomb racks under both wings. VMS-3 was in the Virgin Islands to participate in the neutrality patrol. The rudder has red, white, and blue stripes, and the cowl has the upper half painted white to indicate the second aircraft in the section. (*Tailhook*)

Left: The first aircraft assigned to the new Naval Air Station Jacksonville, Florida, was the Grumman J2F-3 (BuNo 1578), and it is sharing the ramp with a North American SNJ trainer. A Wright R-1830-36 engine driving a three-blade constant-speed prop powered the J2F-3. The J2F-3 is finished in an overall aluminum dope scheme with yellow wing tops. (*Tailhook*)

Below: The Naval Air Station Jacksonville-based J2F-3 is inspected by some civilian dignitaries as the pilot retrieves his parachute off the ground in 1940. The J2F-3 has been fitted with bomb racks under the wings, and a telescopic sight has been placed ahead of the pilot's windshield. Two flight line mechanics, at the side of the aircraft, are preparing to test for water in the aviation fuel. (*Tailhook*)

Above: A pair of Grumman J2F-5 Ducks sits on the flight line at Naval Air Station Whidbey Island, Washington, in 1945. The nearest aircraft (BuNo 60875) has the national insignia painted out to deny enemy gunners an aiming point. The two J2F-5s are used in the utility role. The aircraft are finished overall in an aluminum dope with a flat black anti-glare panel. (*Tailhook*)

Right: A J2F-5 from Utility Squadron 2 (VJ-2) has been fitted with an aerial target-towing reel at the left lower wing root. The aircraft is also armed with a 325-pound depth bomb. A 950-horsepower Wright R-1820-50 radial engine driving a three-blade prop powered the J2F-2. The engine was fitted with a full-chord engine cowling. The aircraft is camouflaged in the NS blue-gray over NS light gray scheme. The rudder has red and white stripes, and the national insignia has the red disc center. (*Real War Photos*)

Below: A Grumman J2F-5 sits on the flight line at Naval Air Station Corpus Christi, Texas, in 1942. Aircraft No. 7 was attached to the base flight and was used in the utility role and an air base hack for pilots. The aircraft is camouflaged in the NS blue-gray over NS light gray with "N.A.S. Corpus Christi" in white. The J2F-5 is equipped with an arrestor hook, enabling it to land on a carrier. (*Tailhook*)

Above: A J2F-5 makes an arrested landing on the escort carrier USS *Charger* (CVE-30) in August 1942. The landing signal officer has turned around to see which wire was caught off the fiddlebars, which hold the wires off the deck. The *Charger* was used during World War II to train Navy aviators in the fine art of landing on a carrier at sea. (*Tailhook*)

Left: A U.S. Coast Guard Grumman J2F-6 is being prepared to be lifted off its cradle aboard the icebreaker USS *Eastwind* (AG-279) off Greenland in 1944. The J2F-6 was used to locate German positions along the coast of the large island. The J2F-6 is camouflaged in the tri-tone measure that consisted of NS sea blue and NS intermediate blue over NS insignia white. (*USCG*)

Below: A Columbia Aircraft J2F-6 (BuNo 36967) flies out over the hills of southern California in 1945. The production of the J2F-6 was transferred to Columbia Aircraft when the U.S. Navy decided that Grumman F6F Hellcats were more important to the war effort than the J2F Ducks. Aircraft 131 is finished in an overall aluminum dope scheme with Navy blue wing tops and has the letter Z on the tail. (*Tailhook*)

Above: A member of the flight crew, probably the flight mechanic, of this U.S. Coast Guard J2F-6 Duck makes an examination of the radial engine. The J2F-6 was assigned to the icebreaker USS *Northwind* (WAG-282) during Operation High Jump, the American incursion into Antarctica in early 1947. The attack transport USS *Yancey* (AKA-93) is in the background. Columbia Aircraft produced the J2F-6 under license from Grumman. (*USCG*)

Right: A U.S. Coast Guard Grumman J4F-1 (V215) is about to be loaded with a 325-pound depth bomb on its right wing at Air Station Brooklyn in 1943. The wing rack could accommodate a depth bomb, conventional bomb, a raft, or other rescue gear. The aircraft is camouflaged in NS blue-gray over NS light gray. The aircraft number, "215," is painted on the nose in white. The U.S. Coast Guard purchased 25 Grumman Widgeons. (*Tailhook*)

Below: A U.S. Coast Guard J4F-1 sits on the flight line at Air Station San Francisco in 1941. The aircraft is finished in an overall aluminum dope with yellow wing tops, the yellow being brought around and under the leading edge of the wing. The U.S. Coast Guard emblem has been placed below the cockpit area. The propellers are wooden and left in a natural finish. (*Tailhook*)

Above: A U.S. Coast Guard J4F-1 flies out of Air Station Port Angeles, Washington, in 1941. The aircraft's serial number, V203, is painted on the fuselage side and under the hull. The rudder is painted in red and white stripes topped by blue. The wing tops are finished in yellow. Following the war, the aircraft was declared surplus, sold in the civilian market, and registered N68361. (*USCG*)

Left: A Grumman JRF-1A Goose operates with Utility Squadron 1 (VJ-1) out of Naval Air Station San Diego, California, in 1939. The aircraft code 1-J-11 and the squadron emblem are on the nose. The vertical stabilizer and horizontal stabilizers are painted willow green. The aircraft is finished overall in aluminum dope with yellow wing tops. The lower hull is painted with a noncorrosive black. (*Tailhook*)

Below: A U.S. Coast Guard JRF-2 is camouflaged in NS blue-gray over NS light gray in 1943. The JRF has been fitted with deicing boots along the leading edges of the wings' vertical and horizontal surfaces for operations in the northern climes. The JRF was the civilian version of the Grumman G-26. (*Tailhook*)

Above: A Grumman JRF-2, camouflaged in the tri-color scheme, flies out over the Rocky Mountains in 1944. The JRF had a wingspan of 49 feet and a length of 36 feet, 6 inches. With an onboard fuel capacity of 220 gallons, the aircraft had a range of 640 miles. The JRF-2 cost the U.S. Coast Guard $79,256 each. The JRF remained in U.S. Coast Guard service until 1954.

Right: A U.S. Coast Guard JRF-2 (V176, serial number 1065) flies out of Air Station Port Angeles, Washington, in 1941. The Pratt & Whitney 450-horsepower R-985-SB-2 powered the JRF-2 and gave the aircraft a maximum speed of 201 mph. V176 crashed off Seattle in April 1943 with the loss of all crew. (*Tailhook*)

Below: A U.S. Coast Guard JRF-3 (V192) rides at buoy in Lake Superior at White Fish Point, Paradise, Michigan, in 1941. The Pratt & Whitney Wasp Junior engines are fitted with two-speed Hamilton-Standard metal propellers. The JRF-3 could be equipped with a single-lens aerial mapping camera. (*USCG*)

Above: A U.S. Navy JRF-5 sits chocked at Naval Air Station Jacksonville in 1942. The JRF-5 was the only Goose to be assigned to the base flight, and it is camouflaged in an unusual NS blue-gray over NS light gray scheme with the paint demarcation line only at the anti-glare panel and the top of the fuselage. The aircraft is fitted with spinners over the Hamilton-Standard props. (*Tailhook*)

Left: A U.S. Coast Guard JRF-5G from Air Station Port Angeles flies out over the Olympia Mountains in Washington in 1943. The -5G was used to designate the 10 U.S. Coast Guard aircraft that were transferred from the U.S. Navy in 1943. The aircraft is fitted with a bomb rack under the right wing, close to the engine nacelle, that could be fitted with a depth bomb or other ordnance. (*USCG*)

Below: A U.S. Navy Grumman JRF-5 shares the ramp with a Martin JM-1 (BuNo 75685) on Guam in 1945. The little Grumman is finished in an overall aluminum dope with oversize national "star and bar" insignia. The JM-1 is painted overall in a bright yellow scheme befitting its role as a high-speed target tug. (*Tailhook*)

Above: An overall gloss Navy blue JRF-5 (BuNo 37803) makes a test flight from the Grumman Aircraft Engineering Corp. in Bethpage, Long Island, New York, in 1945. A pair of Pratt & Whitney Wasp Junior R-985-AN-6 engines with 450 horsepower driving Hamilton-Standard two-blade metal props powered the JRF-5. The "AN" engine designator was for Army-Navy to commonalize the parts between the two services. (*Tailhook*)

Right: U.S. Coast Guard JRF-5G V229 (BuNo 37773) was operating out of Air Station Port Angeles following World War II and was finished in overall aluminum dope with yellow-orange wing panels and fuselage band, edged in black. The Grumman Goose was returned to the U.S. Navy when the U.S. Coast Guard began receiving the Grumman UF-1G/HU-16 Albatross for search-and-rescue operations. (*USCG*)

Below: A Grumman JRF-6 (BuNo 84814) is being warmed up and awaiting the flight crew and passengers from the U.S. Naval Academy, Annapolis, Maryland, in the 1950s. The JRF is painted in an overall gloss Navy blue scheme with all lettering in white. The Naval Academy operated a few JRFs well into the 1960s. (*Tailhook*)

Hall Aluminum Aircraft

The Hall Aluminum Aircraft Co. was given a contract by the U.S. Navy in 1927 to produce a version of the Naval Aircraft Factory (NAF) XPN-11 flying boat to be designated the PH-1. The aircraft were built at a Buffalo, New York, factory that was shared with Consolidated. The collaboration between Ruben Fleet of Consolidated and Charles Hall of Hall Aircraft benefited both of the manufacturers. Consolidated learned the technique of building an all-aluminum aircraft, and Hall got the space to build its aircraft.

Charles M. Hall was credited with developing the electrolytic process that allowed aluminum to be processed more economically. Hall discovered the process in 1886 while working with Pittsburgh Reduction Co., a company he founded with partners. The company would later be named Alcoa. The aircraft industry did not discover aluminum until the need for lightweight engines and airframes became apparent during World War I. Most aircraft during that period were constructed of wood and cloth with a cast iron engine. When Alcoa and NAF developed the process for manufacturing and forming aluminum, the aircraft industry was changed. Aluminum could be used for the airframe, and lightweight radial engines could be produced. This increased speed, extended range, and made structures more stable.

The NAF XPN-11 was a development of the early Curtiss H-12 and H-16 biplane flying boats that were built by the British during World War I and designated the Felixstowe F-5. The Hall XPH-1 would follow the basic design of the XPN-11, but the aircraft would have an all-aluminum hull and a single vertical stabilizer. The XPH-1 made its first flight in December 1929. The U.S. Navy, following flight tests, ordered nine examples of the PH-1. These would be some of the last biplane patrol aircraft built for the U.S. Navy.

The U.S. Coast Guard saw a need for a search-and-rescue aircraft not quite as big as the Consolidated PBY, and in 1936 Hall received an order for seven PH-2s. In 1939, the U.S. Coast Guard ordered an additional seven improved PH-3s. The PH-3 was constructed at the old Keystone-Fleetwings Aircraft facility in Bristol, Pennsylvania.

In 1934, Hall produced a twin float patrol bomber designated the XTBH-1. The high-wing monoplane was powered by a pair of Wright Cyclone R-1820 radial engines. When the engines were changed to Wright XR-1820-60s, the aircraft designator was changed to XPTBH-2. The XPTBH-1 was constructed at the old Fleetwings Aircraft facility. The U.S. Navy showed no interest in a twin-float torpedo bomber, although Heinkel of Germany built the He 115, an aircraft that closely resembled the XPTBH-1 design.

Hall Aircraft will be remembered as a pioneer in the construction of all-metal aircraft and designers of aluminum structures. Hall Aluminum Aircraft was absorbed into Consolidated Aircraft in 1940 and built components for the PBY Catalina during World War II.

A U.S. Coast Guard Hall PH-2 flying boat (V165) has been rolled out of the hangar at Air Station St. Petersburg, Albert Whitted Airport, in 1938. The Hall Boat is fitted with beaching gear to enable it to be maneuvered on land. All U.S. Coast Guard aircraft were finished in an overall aluminum dope, with orange-yellow wing tops. V165 was lost in 1938 while on a medical mission in the Gulf of Mexico. (*USCG*)

Above: A Hall PH-2 (V164) flies out over the Atlantic in 1939. V164 was on a rescue mission to the ketch *Atlantis* out of Air Station Brooklyn, New York, on 15 July 1939. Following the pickup of a stricken sailor, the PH-2 was attempting to take off when the aircraft exploded and sank with the loss of one crewman. (*USCG*)

Right: A U.S. Coast Guard PH-2 (V164) is in the water and secured to the seaplane ramp at Air Station Cape May, New Jersey, in early 1939. A pair of Wright Cyclone 875-horsepower R-1820F-51 engines powered the Hall PH-2. With an onboard fuel capacity of 892 gallons, the flying boat had a range of 2,242 miles. (*USCG*)

Below: V164, a Hall PH-2, sits on beaching gear at Air Station Brooklyn, New York, on 7 March 1939. The U.S. Coast Guard serial number V164 has been painted on the bottom of the hull, to be read from the left underside. The Hall Boats had a wingspan of 72 feet, 10 inches, and they had a maximum gross takeoff weight of 16,450 pounds. (*USCG*)

Above: Three Hall PH-3s, V178 from Air Station San Diego and V180 and V181 from Air Station San Francisco, California, fly in a trail formation in 1941. The U.S. Coast Guard purchased seven PH-3 flying boats, with three of them going to the Pacific coast. The PH-3 featured full cowling over the Wright Cyclone radial engines, and Hamilton Standard constant-speed props were added. (*Tailhook*)

Left: A Hall PH-2 (V166) sits on the ramp at Air Station, Biloxi, Mississippi, in 1939. V166 served at Biloxi and Air Station San Diego, California, from 1939 to 1944. The V166 and its crew were responsible for rescuing 21 Norwegian sailors when a German U-boat torpedoed their oil tanker in July 1942. The V166 participated in many other rescues in the Gulf of Mexico. (*USCG*)

Below: The first Hall PH-3 (V177) was commissioned by the U.S. Coast Guard at Air Station Brooklyn, New York, in January 1941, and it served there until it was decommissioned in March 1944. The PH-3 Hall Boat had a maximum speed of 155 mph and a stall speed of 61 mph. The PH-3 could be armed with up to five .30-caliber machine guns and four 325-pound depth bombs. (*USCG*)

Above: A U.S. Coast Guard PH-3 camouflaged in NS blue-gray over NS light gray taxis up to a seaplane ramp in 1943. A crewman from the PH-3 is standing in the nose gunner's position ready to catch a line from the shore. The beaching gear will soon be attached and the aircraft brought ashore and made ready for its next search-and-rescue mission. (*Tailhook*)

Right: The Hall Aluminum XPTBH-1 (BuNo 9721) was constructed at the Fleetwings facility in Bristol, Pennsylvania. Following an engine change to 800-horsepower Pratt & Whitney XR-1830-60 engines, the designator was changed to XPTBH-2. The aircraft had fabric-covered wings, an all-aluminum fuselage, and twin floats. (*National Archives*)

Below: The XPTBH-2 was flown to the Naval Test Center at Anacostia, Maryland, in 1937 where it was tested. The top speed was rated at 186 mph, and it could carry two torpedoes and a crew of four. The U.S. Navy decided on the Douglas TBD-1 torpedo bomber instead of the Hall Aluminum torpedo bomber. (*Tailhook*)

Martin Aircraft

Glenn Luther Martin founded Martin Aircraft in 1912 in Santa Anna, California. The Martin Co. employed many of the early aviation pioneers, including Bill Boeing, Donald Douglas, and James McDonnell. Some of the early Martin designs were trainers for the U.S. Army that were designed by Donald Douglas.

In 1917, the Martin Co. moved to Ohio and in 1929 moved to Baltimore, Maryland. While in Ohio, it produced bombers for the U.S. Army and seaplanes for the U.S. Navy. The Baltimore factory was the most modern facility, and it was designed to produce all-metal aircraft. The Martin PM-1 flying boat was ordered in quantity, and it employed Alclad aluminum in the structure. Martin also produced a Consolidated flying boat by underbidding Consolidated, starting a rivalry that would last for more than 30 years.

The Glenn L. Martin Aircraft Co. produced three different flying boat designs employed by the U.S. Navy during World War II. The three Martin M-130 Clippers were purchased by Pan Am in 1935 and used on its Pacific routes. When World War II broke out in the Pacific, the U.S. Navy pressed into service the two remaining clippers, the Philippine Clipper and the China Clipper, the Hawaii Clipper having been lost without a trace in 1936 on a flight from Guam to Manila. The M-130 was a four-engine high-wing monoplane with sponsons called "sea wings" located at cabin level that served two functions: to stabilize the plane on water and to store fuel. The Philippine Clipper was lost in 1943 when it hit a mountain while attempting to land at San Francisco, and the China Clipper crashed at Port of Spain, Trinidad, in 1945. The two U.S. Navy M-130s operated with Pan Am crews in civilian markings, allowing them to enter neutral ports.

In 1937, Martin engineers began working on a new patrol bomber design that would be known as the PBM Mariner. First, they designed and built a three-eighths-scale flying model. The Martin M-162A, called the Tadpole Clipper, was used to test the aerodynamics and hydrodynamics of the design. The scale aircraft was powered by a pair of Chevrolet four-cylinder engines mounted in the fuselage driving the two props via a drive V belt. The M-162A had fixed floats and a nondihedral horizontal stabilizer. Following successful flight tests, the U.S. Navy placed an order for a single Martin M-162, to be designated the XPBM-1. The XPBM-1 was a large twin-engine patrol bomber that was powered by a pair of Wright R-2600-6 radial engines producing 1,600 horsepower for takeoff. The engines were mounted at the break of the dihedral gull-shaped wings. The wing-mounted floats were retractable, and the horizontal stabilizer was without dihedral, a feature that would be changed on the production PBM-1.

The U.S. Navy was satisfied with the design and ordered 20 PBM-1s, now named Mariner. The aircraft were divided between Patrol Squadrons 55 and 56 (VP-55 and VP-56) between 1940 and 1941. The PBM-1s were soon flying in the Atlantic on neutrality patrol, protecting American shipping interests. The PBM-1 was armed with five .50-caliber machine guns, one in the powered nose turret, one each in the waist positions, and one in the dorsal and tail turrets. A 20 mm cannon was considered for the nose turret but was never fitted.

A single XPBM-2, an ex-PBM-1, was constructed, and it had fuel capacity increased from 2,700 gallons to 4,800 gallons. The XPBM-2 had a strengthened fuselage to allow it to be catapulted from a barge. The tests were successful, but the U.S. Navy offered no contracts. The XPBM-2 served as a test aircraft until 1944.

The U.S. Navy was so impressed with the PBM-1 that it placed an order for 379 of the improved PBM-3s and even helped finance a new factory at Middle River, Maryland, outside of Baltimore. The PBM-3 had powered nose and tail turrets, fixed wing-mounted floats, and enlarged engine nacelles to

A steward on the Martin M-130 China Clipper stands in the entry door. The M-130 was operated by Pan American Airways Systems on its Pacific route before the beginning of World War II. The M-130 cruised at 150 mph and had a range of 3,200 miles carrying 41 passengers. The U.S. Navy bought the M-130 and contracted with Pan Am to operate the aircraft. (SAM)

handle a greater bomb load. The engines were upgraded to 1,700-horsepower Wright R-2600-12 radials. Range was rated at 3,100 miles at patrol speed. Only 32 PBM-3s were constructed. The rest of the Navy order was for the PBM-3R, a transport version, and the PBM-3C an up-armed PBM with twin nose and tail .50-caliber machine guns. A single XPBM-3E was constructed to test the new H2X sea search radar that was mounted atop the fuselage. The PBM-3S was a stripped-down version that was used to hunt U-boats in the Atlantic. All .50-caliber machine guns were removed and replaced with fake guns, and the internal armor was removed.

As production continued on the PBM-3, an engine and propeller change brought about the new designation PBM-3D. The engines were the 1,900-horsepower Wright R-2600-22 radials with four-blade props. A total of 259 PBM-3Ds were constructed, with most having been fitted with air search radar atop the fuselage.

The PBM-5 was an improved version of the PBM-3 series with Wright 2,100-horsepower R-2600-34s and four-blade props. A total of 628 PBM-5s were constructed, and many were further converted to PBM-5S and PBM-5G for the U.S. Coast Guard. The -5S and -5G versions were essentially the same. An amphibian version was constructed after World War II. The PBM-5A had retractable tricycle gear installed. A total of 36 PBM-5As were constructed. The PBM Mariner served through the Korean War until it was replaced by the Martin P5M Marlin in U.S. Navy and U.S. Coast Guard service.

The last Martin flying boats produced by the Glenn L. Martin Aircraft Co. were the XPB2M-1 Mars and the JRM-1 Mars. The prototype XPB2M-1 Mars was ordered in 1938 and completed and first flown in 1941. The XPB2M-1 was the largest flying boat built at the time of rollout. The Hughes (HK-1) H-4 "Spruce Goose" was the largest flying boat ever built and flown. The XPB2M-1 had a wingspan of 200 feet and a maximum gross takeoff weight of 75,570 pounds. Powered by Wright 18-cylinder R-3350-18 engines that produced 2,200 horsepower, the Mars had a maximum speed of just faster than 200 mph. The U.S. Navy decided that it needed transport aircraft more than a large patrol bomber, and the prototype Mars was converted to a transport.

The Martin JRM-1 Mars was a modified version of XPB2M-1 Mars, now referred to as the Old Lady. A total of 20 JRM-1s were ordered, but with the war in the Pacific coming to an end, only six were completed. The JRM-1 was powered by four Wright R-3350-8 Duplex Cyclone engines, and the twin tails were replaced with a single vertical stabilizer. The first JRM-1, called the Hawaiian Mars, was completed in June 1945, with the Philippine Mars, Marianas Mars, Marshall Mars, and Hawaiian Mars II following. The original Hawaiian Mars was lost in 1945 in the Chesapeake Bay. A final version of the Mars was the JRM-2 Caroline Mars. The JRM-2 was powered by four Pratt & Whitney R-4360 four-row radials with 3,000 horsepower. All of the JRM-1 and -2 models were brought up to JRM-3 standards with changes to internal configurations to increase cargo and passenger capacity.

The JRM Mars would become the world's largest water bombers when they were converted by adding a 6,000-gallon water tank and a pair of water scoops. The water bombers went to work in 1960 putting out forest fires in Canada. Accidents claimed the Marianas Mars and the Caroline Mars. The two remaining aircraft were purchased by Coulson Aircrane.

Martin Aircraft merged with the Marietta Company in 1961, and in 1993 acquired the General Dynamics Co. aerospace division. In 1995, the Martin-Marietta Co. and Lockheed Aircraft combined to create Lockheed Martin.

Above: The M-130 China Clipper was assigned the bureau number 48231 and flown in the Pan Am color scheme with civilian markings NC14716, which allowed the aircraft to enter neutral ports during wartime. The M-130 had a wingspan of 130 feet and a maximum gross weight of 52,000 pounds. Three Martin M130s were built, Hawaii Clipper, Philippines Clipper, and China Clipper. (*SAM*)

Right: A flying scale model of the Martin PBM was constructed to test-flight characteristics. The model M-162A was built and flown in 1937 from the Glenn L. Martin facility in Baltimore, Maryland. The trolley was constructed of wood and has what appear to be Ford Model T wheels. The M-162A was constructed to three-eighths scale with twin Chevrolet engines in the fuselage powering the twin props. (*Tailhook*)

Below: The prototype XPBM-1 (BuNo 0796), Martin Model 162, was first flown in 1939 with a straight horizontal stabilizer. The aircraft had gull wings, retractable wing floats, and twin vertical stabilizers. The prototype was painted in an overall aluminum dope scheme with orange-yellow wing tops. The XPBM-1 would serve as the test bed for the XPBM-1A, the amphibian version of the Mariner. (*Tailhook*)

Above: The production line at the Glenn L. Martin facility in Baltimore is busy producing the 20 PBM-1s for U.S. Navy patrol squadrons in 1941. The PBM-1 Mariner in the foreground appears to be almost complete, lacking only the cowling around the 1,200-horsepower Wright R-2600-6 radial engines. The reason for the amphibian on the assembly floor is unknown. (*Tailhook*)

Left: The third production PBM-1 (BuNo 1249) has been assigned to Patrol Squadron 55 (VP-55) and assigned aircraft number 9 (55P9) in 1941. The aircraft is painted overall in an aluminum dope scheme with orange-yellow wing tops. The lower half of the engine cowling is painted insignia red to indicate the third aircraft in the third section. (*Tailhook*)

Below: The Martin PBM-1 was armed with four .50-caliber machine guns, one in the nose and dorsal turrets and a single hand-held weapon in the waist gunner's positions. In addition, the Mariner could be armed with up to 5,200 pounds of bombs in the engine nacelle bomb bays. The PBM-1 could also carry two 2,000-pound torpedoes in lieu of bombs. A crew of seven was required to operate the PBM-1. (*Tailhook*)

Above: The first production PBM-1, serving with Patrol Squadron 55 (VP-55), is swung aboard the seaplane tender USS *Albemarle* (AV-5) in 1941. The aircraft is painted overall aluminum dope with orange-yellow wing tops. The fuselage band, cowlings, prop warning stripes, and command chevron are insignia red. The black spinners were fitted to a few PBM-1s. The PBM-1 has a neutrality star on the nose, and the commander's aircraft is operating out of Puerto Rico in early 1942. (*Tailhook*)

Right: A PBM-1 serving with Patrol Squadron 56 (VP-56) taxis from Middle River, Maryland, before a test flight in 1941. The retractable floats greatly reduced drag but added weight for the retracting mechanism. A neutrality star has been added to the nose of the PBM-1. The United States officially initiated the neutrality patrol on 5 September 1939 in the waters off the Caribbean Islands and 200 miles off the coast of North and South America. (*Tailhook*)

Below: A PBM-1 serving with VP-56 flies over the Pimlico Race Track, north of the Martin, Baltimore, Maryland, facility in 1941. Both VP-55 and VP-56 received production models of the PBM-1 in 1941. Glenn L. Martin moved his production facility from California to Ohio and then to Maryland in 1929. This PBM-1, 56P6, carries a neutrality star on the nose. (*Tailhook*)

Above: A U.S. Army guard with an M-1 Garand rifle at parade rest by a covered water-cooled .50-caliber machine gun at a seaplane base at the Naval Seaplane Base, Naval Air Station Bermuda, in 1942. The PBM-1 is assigned to Patrol Squadron 74 (VP-74) and is camouflaged in the NS blue-gray over NS light gray scheme with red and white tail stripes. VP-55 was redesignated as VP-74 on 1 July 1941. A Vought OS2U Kingfisher is flying over the harbor. (*Tailhook*)

Left: Aircraft No. 22 leads a flight of two PBM-1s ahead of a pair of the newer PBM-3 Mariners in 1942. The PBM-3 could be distinguished from the older PBM-1 by the wing-mounted floats. The aircraft are probably from Patrol Squadron 74 (VP-74), the ex-VP-55 that pioneered the use of the Mariner in squadron service. The Pratt & Whitney R-2600-12 1,700-horsepower twin-row radial engine powered the PBM-3. (*Tailhook*)

Below: Aircraft No. 2, a PBM-1 from VP-74 (74P2), makes an overland flight in early 1942. The aircraft is camouflaged in a NS blue-gray over NS light gray scheme with a small national insignia on the nose. The PBM-1s from VP-74 operated in the Atlantic, based out of Norfolk, Virginia, with forward operating bases in Iceland and Puerto Rico. (*Tailhook*)

Above: A less-than-factory-fresh PBM-3C (BuNo 6505) flies on a patrol in 1943. The upper wings show the effects of high-octane aviation fuel staining. A total of 274 of the -3 models were built, and they had upgraded power turrets with the addition of a power tail turret, all still armed with a single .50-caliber machine gun. This aircraft is camouflaged in the NS blue-gray over NS light gray scheme. (*Tailhook*)

Right: A PBM-3C is washed down following a landing in salt water in 1943. The aircraft is being guarded by an armed sailor carrying an M-1903 Springfield rifle, all under the watchful eye of a Navy chief. The PBM is sitting on beaching gear to enable it to be moved from the water up the seaplane ramp. The oil cooler on the PBM-3 Pratt & Whitney engines was moved to below the engine cowling. (*Tailhook*)

Below: A PBM-3C sits at buoy in 1943 at a seaplane base somewhere in the Pacific. It was customary to moor the seaplanes in the water, ferry the crew to the aircraft, and bring the aircraft ashore for maintenance. Aircraft No. 3 is camouflaged in the NS blue-gray over NS light gray scheme. The buoy was painted black and white for recognition. (*Tailhook*)

Above: As the aircraft commander watches, the flight mechanic tugs at the mooring line to release this late-production PBM-3C from its buoy at Kerama Retto Island on 30 March 1945. The Mariner aircraft was camouflaged in the tri-tone scheme authorized in 1943. A surface search radar is fitted on the forward fuselage just aft of the cockpit. The nose turret contains one .50-caliber machine gun. (*Real War Photos*)

Left: A PBM-5E is being hoisted out of the water onto the deck of a seaplane tender at Kerama Retto Island on 17 May 1945. The aircraft, named Rectum, had "some disagreement" with a Japanese anti-aircraft gunner that caused some serious damage to its left wing float and horizontal stabilizer. The crew of the Mariner has received an engineering "E" award. The AN/APS-15 surface search radar is atop the fuselage, and the PBM-5E is armed with eight .50-caliber machine guns. (*Real War Photos*)

Below: A PBM-5G from the Air Sea Rescue Service, aircraft ASR-13, was still carrying the Atlantic gull-gray and white scheme when operated by the U.S. Coast Guard. The Mariner had all of the armor and gun turrets removed to save weight and extend the range. The wing center section is painted yellow to increase visibility from above. (*USCG*)

Above: An overall aluminum dope-painted PBM-5C operates over land after World War II. The aircraft has orange-yellow panels edged in black on the wingtips and an orange-yellow fuselage band edged in black. The floats are yellow, and the surface search radar and anti-glare panel is flat black. The U.S. Coast Guard emblem is placed below the cockpit. (*USCG*)

Right: The crew of this U.S. Coast Guard PBM-5G (BuNo 84732) practices retrieving survivors from a raft. A crew member of the Mariner standing on the top of the fuselage is filming the training exercise. A football-shaped direction finder antenna is located on the aft fuselage just above the rear crew hatch. The rear power turret has been replaced by a rear observer position fitted with a clear Plexiglas bubble. (*USCG*)

Below: A U.S. Coast Guard PBM-5G (BuNo 84732), aircraft R-22, taxis. The PBM-5Gs were former U.S. Navy PBM-5s or -5S's that were given to the U.S. Coast Guard to replace its PBM-3C models. The Pratt & Whitney Double Wasp R-2800-34 with a four-blade prop powered the PBM-5G. The U.S. Coast Guard replaced its PBMs with the Martin P5M Marlin, a design based on the PBM with a modified hull, nose, and tail. (*USCG*)

Above: A U.S. Coast Guard PBM-5G (BuNo 84732) demonstrates a jet-assisted takeoff (JATO) in late 1940. The JATO units allowed the PBM to take off with higher gross weight or shorten the takeoff run in rough seas. R-22 is painted overall in aluminum dope with orange-yellow floats and panels outlined in black on the wingtips. The fuselage stripe is also orange-yellow with black outlines. (*USCG*)

Left: The prototype Martin Mars XPB2M-1 takes a test flight in 1942. The Mars was the largest flying boat to be flown by the U.S. Navy in World War II. The Model 170 was powered by the Wright Duplex R-3350 twin-row radial engine. The Mars was painted overall in aluminum dope with chrome yellow wing tops. The XPB2M-1 was converted to a transport and redesignated XPB2M-1R as the prototype for the JRM Mars. (*Tailhook*)

Below: The JRM-2 Caroline Mars (BuNo 76824) is tied up at the seaplane base Naval Air Station Jacksonville, Florida, on 15 July 1949. The JRM was a development of the XPB2M-1 Mars with a single vertical stabilizer replacing the twin tail. The U.S. Navy determined that the Mars craft were more important as transports than patrol bombers. The JRM-2 had a higher gross weight rating than the JRM-1. Six JRMs were constructed out of the 20 that were originally ordered. (*Tailhook*)

Above: The Marianas Mars, a JRM-1 (BuNo 76821), was assigned to the Naval Air Transport Service following World War II. The JRM was powered by four Wright 2,300-horsepower R-3350-8 18-cylinder air-cooled radial engines. The JRMs were all painted in an overall gloss Navy blue scheme. All of the JRM Mars planes were assigned to Transport Squadron 2 (VR-2) at Naval Air Station Alameda, California. (*Tailhook*)

Right: Four Mars craft fly in left trail echelon formation, led by Philippine Mars (BuNo 76821), followed by Marianas Mars (BuNo 76821). One sister, the Marshall Mars (BuNo 76822), was destroyed by fire off Honolulu, Hawaii, on 5 April 1950, and Hawaiian Mars (BuNo 76819) was lost on 5 August 1945. The JRM-1 had a payload capacity of up to 32 tons, and the JRM-2 had a capacity of 40 tons. All remaining Mars were brought to -3 standards with strengthened load floors. (*Tailhook*)

Below: The Philippine Mars (BuNo 76820) sits tied up at buoy at Naval Air Station Jacksonville, Florida, in 1948. The side cargo door is being used to load cargo and personnel. The tail code RA was assigned to Transport Squadron 2 (VR-2). The JRM-2 could carry up to 132 passengers or up to 40 tons of cargo or a combination of both. The aircraft had provisions to be brought on land for maintenance, but the JRM spent most of its time in the water. (*Tailhook*)

Naval Air Factory

The Naval Aircraft Factory (NAF) was established at the Navy yard on the Delaware River in Philadelphia, Pennsylvania, in 1917. The NAF was built to produce U.S. Navy aircraft during the World War I when the Navy could not interest aircraft manufacturers to produce aircraft for it. By law, the U.S. Navy could produce up to 10 percent of its required aircraft.

When the factory was completed in 1917, the NAF set about constructing the Curtiss H-16 flying boat that would be used to patrol the Atlantic, searching for German U-boats. The first two H-16s were sent to Killingholme, England, to began patrol duties. The English made some modifications and improvements to the H-16 and designated them the Felixstowe F-5. The NAF produced a version of the F-5 designated as the F-5-L.

The NAF also produced the N3N Canary, the trainer that became known as the Yellow Peril to U.S. Navy aviation cadets. The OS2N, the NAF version of the Vought-Sikorsky OS2U-3 Kingfisher, was also produced at the NAF. The NAF also produced the SBN, a scout bomber that had been designed by Brewster Aircraft. The SBN had been used by Torpedo Squadron 8 (VT-8) in the USS *Hornet* (CV-8) while it waited for its Douglas TBD Devastators.

The U.S. Navy relied heavily on the Consolidated PBY patrol bomber, and when too few of them were coming from Consolidated and Boeing, it turned to the NAF for production.

The PBN-1 Nomad was a modified version of the PBY-5 with a noticeably taller vertical stabilizer and a lengthened and modified hull shape. The bow turret was enlarged with a .50-caliber machine gun replacing the .30-caliber machine gun. The wingtip floats were redesigned, and the wing was strengthened to handle additional underwing stores.

A total of 156 Nomads were produced , with 138 going to the Soviet Union and the rest going to the U.S. Navy for use at Naval Air Station Whidbey Island, Washington, to train crews for service in Alaska. Consolidated used the PBN-1 design on its PBY-6A, an amphibian version. The PBY-6A had a sea search radar atop the cockpit area, a shorter hull, and a bow turret that contained a pair of .30-caliber machine guns.

In 1945, the Naval Aircraft Factory was closed, disestablished, and converted to the Naval Surface Warfare Center, which aids in the design of surface ship systems.

The Naval Aircraft Factory (NAF) Philadelphia, Pennsylvania, produced a version of the Consolidated PBY-5 Catalina called the PBN-1 Nomad. The NAF produced 156 PBN-1s, with 138 given to the Soviet Union. The PBN-1 had a modified hull with a 2-foot extension, redesigned wing floats, a new bow turret with one .50-caliber machine gun, and additional fuel in the center section. (*Real War Photos*)

The NAF PBN-1 is camouflaged in a modified tri-tone scheme in 1945. The PBN-1 was used at Naval Air Station Whidbey Island to train crews that would be used in the Alaska area of operation. The PBN-1 has underwing Yagi radar and weapons shackles. Clamshell-type doors cover the bomb-aiming window just below the bow-mounted turret. The PBY-6 type tail and modified hull was a recognition feature of the NAF PBN-1. (*Tailhook*)

Sikorsky Aircraft

Igor Sikorsky, although better known for designing the first practical helicopter, also produced flying boats for the U.S. Navy. Born in Russia, Sikorsky produced aircraft for Russia and France before immigrating to New York in 1919. Fascinated with vertical flight, but requiring money to produce it, Sikorsky began designing and building aircraft for Pan Am. The S-38 amphibian became the original Clipper, and it was used to prove routes pioneered by Pan Am to Central and South America.

The U.S. Navy procured a military version of the S-38, designated the XPS-1, and followed up with the XPS-2 and -3 models. The S-38 series was a twin-engine, twin-boom amphibian that could seat up to 10 passengers. Sikorsky also produced an experimental patrol bomber, the XP2S-1 twin-engine flying boat, which was armed with two .30-caliber machine guns and two 500-pound bombs.

Sikorsky produced four aircraft types that were used by the U.S. Navy during World War II, with only one, the XPBS-1, originally ordered by the U.S. Navy. The others were pressed into service. In 1932, Pan Am ordered three Sikorsky S-42 flying boats, followed by four S-42As and three S-42Bs. The aircraft were powered by four Pratt & Whitney S5B1-G Hornet engines. When World War II broke out, at least one S-42 was pressed into U.S. Navy service and assigned to Transport Squadron 1 (VR-1). It was used in the Atlantic and camouflaged in NS blue-gray over NS light gray.

The Japanese liked the S-42 design so much they stole the design technical plans and construction drawings when a delegation was visiting the Short Aircraft factory in England. The Kawanishi H6K, Type 97, Allied code named Mavis, bore an uncanny resemblance to the Sikorsky S-42 when it first appeared in Japanese naval service in 1936.

In 1935, Sikorsky offered its Model S-43 to the U.S. Navy as a utility transport. Designated JRS-1, a total of 17 were constructed, with 15 going to the U.S. Navy and originally assigned to Utility Squadron 1 (VJ-1) and two going to the U.S. Marine Corps, one each assigned to Marine Utility Squadrons 1 and 2 (VMJ-1 and VMJ-2). The Japanese attack on Pearl Harbor on 7 December 1941 caught one of the U.S. Marine Corps JRS-1s (BuNo 1061) from VMJ-2 on the tarmac, and it was destroyed by fire. The U.S. Navy JRS-1s were serving with the Naval Base Defense Force, Ford Island, Pearl Harbor, when the Japanese attacked. All survived to be fitted with bomb racks and used as patrol bombers, many searching for the Japanese naval task force.

In 1935, Sikorsky offered its design for a large heavily armed flying boat in response to a U.S. Navy request. The XPBS-1 was the Sikorsky Model VS-44, Vought and Sikorsky having been merged by United Aircraft, and it was called the Flying Dreadnought. The XPBS-1 was armed with .50-caliber machine guns, .30-caliber machine guns, and up to 4,000 pounds of bombs. The XPBS-1 was powered by four Pratt & Whitney R-1830-68 Twin-Wasp engines that produced 900 horsepower each. Following flight testing in 1937, the entry from Consolidated, the PB2Y-1 Coronado, was chosen as the new U.S. Navy four-engine patrol bomber. The XPBS-1 was assigned to Transport Squadron 2 (VR-2) and used in the Pacific out of Naval Air Station Alameda, California, until it was destroyed in a crash in San Francisco Bay in 1942.

Sikorsky produced three of its VS-44As for American Export Airline in 1940. The VS-44A was the civilian version of the U.S. Navy XPBS-1, with all military-related equipment removed. The nose turret was faired over, the tail turret was removed and faired over, and additional windows were installed in the hull. The gloss black and white VS-44As were taken over by the U.S. Navy in January 1942 and operated in the Atlantic and South American routes. The U.S. Navy designated the VS-44A as the JR2S-1 and camouflaged the Excalibur, Excambian, and Exeter in NS blue-gray over NS light gray. It operated them in civilian markings. The Excambian survives and can be seen at the New England Air Museum. The Excalibur was destroyed in 1943 off Newfoundland, Canada.

Following the war, Sikorsky turned his complete attention to building helicopters, his first love. Today, Sikorsky Aircraft continues as a member of United Technologies and builds helicopters that are used around the world, both in civilian and military applications.

A Sikorsky Aircraft S-43 runs up the No. 1 Pratt & Whitney 750-horsepower R-1690-52 radial engine. The S-43 flying boat was known as a "baby clipper" and was being evaluated for possible U.S. Navy service in 1935. The Sikorsky flying boat could accommodate 18 passengers and a crew of three. Pan American was the primary user of the S-43, using them on flights to Cuba. (*Tailhook*)

The first S-43 taken on charge was given the designation JRS-1 (BuNo 0504), and it served as the commander's aircraft for Utility Squadron 1 (VJ-1). It had the side marking of 1-J-1. The JRS-1 had a willow green tail and insignia red engine cowlings. The aircraft was finished overall in aluminum dope with yellow-orange wing tops. (*United Technologies*)

JRS-1 was stationed with Utility Squadron 1 (VJ-1) at Naval Air Station San Diego in 1940. The black area on the lower fuselage and floats was an anti-corrosion/anti-fouling paint. As the JRS-1 was classified as a transport, no offensive or defensive armament was carried. The JRS-1 had a wingspan of 86 feet. (*Tailhook*)

Above: A JRS-1 (I-J-1) flies in formation with another JRS-1 in 1940 over San Diego. A leader's insignia red band has been painted on the aft fuselage. The prop spinners are painted black, as is the lower hull of the flying boat. The squadron would soon be moved to Pearl Harbor, Territory of Hawaii, as war clouds were forming in the Pacific. (*Tailhook*)

Right: An in-flight shot shows a Sikorsky JRS-1 (I-J-5) from Utility Squadron 1 (VJ-1). The JRS was 51 feet 2 inches long and 17 feet 8 inches tall. The maximum takeoff weight was 19,096 pounds, and the maximum speed was 190 mph. Its service ceiling was 20,700 feet. (*Tailhook*)

Below: A JRS-1 (I-J-5) sits on the ramp at Naval Air Station San Diego, California, in 1940. The top half of the engine cowlings are painted white to indicate the No. 5 aircraft assigned to the squadron. A pitot tube extends out of the cockpit roof. The JRS-1 was constructed of aluminum with fabric-covered moveable surfaces. (*Tailhook*)

Above: Four JRS-1 flying boats sit on the Naval Air Station San Diego, California, ramp in 1940. The top half of the engine cowlings on the first craft was painted true blue to indicate the second aircraft in the third section. The undersides of the wings also have the aircraft number painted on them in black. The prop tips are painted, from the tip, red, yellow, and blue. (*Tailhook*)

Left: JRS-1 aircraft 1-J-2 and 1-J-3 are staged on the ramp at Naval Air Station San Diego, California, ready for flight. The yellow-orange wing tops can just be seen at the leading edge of the wing. The top half of the engine cowlings on 1-J-2 are painted insignia red, and the lower half on 1-J-3 is also insignia red. (*Tailhook*)

Below: The U.S. Marine Corps operated this JRS-1 (BuNo 1061) in the then-standard colors of aluminum dope on the fuselage and underwing with the wing top yellow-orange. The JRS-1 served with Marine Corps Utility Squadron 2 (MJ-2), and it was the No. 4 aircraft in the squadron. BuNo 1061 was destroyed by fire when the Japanese attacked Ewa Marine Corps Air Station on 7 December 1941. (*Tailhook*)

Above: A JRS-1 is being held before powering down its engines following a patrol flight out of Pearl Harbor in late 1941. Aircraft No. 9 was one of nine that were stationed with Naval Base Defense Air Force, Ford Island, Pearl Harbor, when the Japanese attacked. They were not damaged and were immediately pressed into service as patrol bombers armed with 325-pound depth bombs. A gunner's position was also fitted to the dorsal fuselage area armed with a .30-caliber machine gun. (*Tailhook*)

Right: A pair of JRS-1s share the ramp at Ford Island, Pearl Harbor, in early 1942, with Grumman J2F Ducks and Vought-Sikorsky OS2U Kingfishers. A Grumman JRF-1 has just landed on the Ford Island runway and is taxiing to the taxi strip. Following the Japanese attacks, revetments were constructed to protect the aircraft. (*Tailhook*)

Below: This JRS-1, 4-J-10, served with Utility Squadron 4 (VJ-4), Utility Wing, Atlantic, Squantum, Massachusetts, in 1942. Its camouflage is NS blue-gray over NS light gray. The propeller blades are painted black, with the tips painted yellow. The JRS-1 served with the U.S. Navy until 1945, when all of them were declared surplus. (*Tailhook*)

Above: Sikorsky Aircraft offered its Model S-44 to the U.S. Navy for evaluation in 1938. The aircraft was accepted for tests, designated XPBS-1, and assigned the bureau number 9995. The National Advisory Committee for Aeronautics (NACA) undertook flight tests in July 1939. NACA was the forerunner of NASA (National Aeronautics and Space Administration). (*NACA*)

Left: The XPBS-1 performs taxiing tests in Long Island Sound off Connecticut in 1939. The XPBS-1 was powered by four Pratt & Whitney 1,050-horsepower R-1830 Hornet radial engines. Armament was to be two .30-caliber and two .50-caliber machine guns and the capacity to carry up to 4,000 pounds of bombs. (*Tailhook*)

Below: The XPBS-1 makes a takeoff run during testing that took place in 1939. The XPBS-1 had a wingspan of 124 feet, a length of 79 feet, and a maximum takeoff weight of 57,500 pounds. Its normal range with 3,900 gallons of fuel was 3,800 miles. (*Tailhook*)

Above: The XPBS-1 is "up on the step" and about to break free of the water. The tail gunner position can clearly be seen at this angle, as can the two dorsal gunners' positions that were covered by sliding hatches. The other gun position was the large bow turret. Armament consisted of a .50-caliber machine gun in the bow and tail position and .30-caliber machine guns in the dorsal gunners' positions. (*Tailhook*)

Right: The XPBS-1 sits on the ramp at Stratford, Connecticut, during testing in 1939. The XPBS-1 was painted overall in aluminum dope with the wing tops in yellow-orange. The black on the lower hull was for corrosion control and anti-fouling. Its maximum speed was 190 mph. Following tests, the U.S. Navy decided that factory space at Vought-Sikorsky could be better used for other projects. The sole XPBS-1 served with Transport Squadron 2 (VR-2) in the Pacific, carrying much-needed supplies and high-value personnel. (*Tailhook*)

Below: American Export Airlines ordered three Vought Sikorsky VS-44A Clippers, the civilian version of the XPBS-1, in 1941, but they were completed as XJR2S-1s and taken over by the U.S. Navy. The three aircraft were assigned civilian registry numbers NC41880 through NC41882, and U.S. Navy bureau numbers 12390 through 12392. As delivered, the three aircraft were named Excalibur, Excambian, and Exeter, and painted in a gloss black and aluminum dope scheme. (*Igor Sikorsky Historical Archives*)

Above: The second JR2S-1 (BuNo 12391), Excambian, carrying civilian registry NC41881 on the underside of the lower wing, upper right wing, and on both sides of the vertical stabilizer, was camouflaged in the standard U.S. Navy scheme of NS blue-gray over NS light gray with an American flag on the forward fuselage. (*Igor Sikorsky Historical Archives*)

Left: Following World War II, the second JR2S-1 was released by the U.S. Navy, redesignated VS-44A, purchased by Avalon Airlines, and painted gloss black and white. The other two VS-44As were also purchased by Avalon Airlines and operated in the Pacific. One example, the Excambian, survives and can be seen at the New England Air Museum, Windsor Locks, Connecticut. (*Igor Sikorsky Historical Archives*)

Below: The U.S. Navy purchased a Sikorsky S-42 Clipper to be used in the Atlantic and Caribbean and operated by a Pan Am crew. The S-42 was camouflaged in the NS blue-gray over NS light gray scheme in 1942. The S-42 was assigned to Transport Squadron 1 (VR-1). The Japanese stole the plans for the S-42, and Kawanishi produced a version, the H6K, Type 97, code name Mavis. (*National Archives*)

ISBN-13 : 978-0-89747-556
ISBN-10 : 0-89747-556-9

9 780897 475563

Squadron Signal
Publications

MIRACLE BABY

STORY & SCREENPLAY BY:

Natzee AB